Unless Recalled Earlier

DATE DUE

DEMCO, INC. 38-2931

Modern Middle East Nations

AND THEIR STRATEGIC PLACE IN THE WORLD

MOROCCO

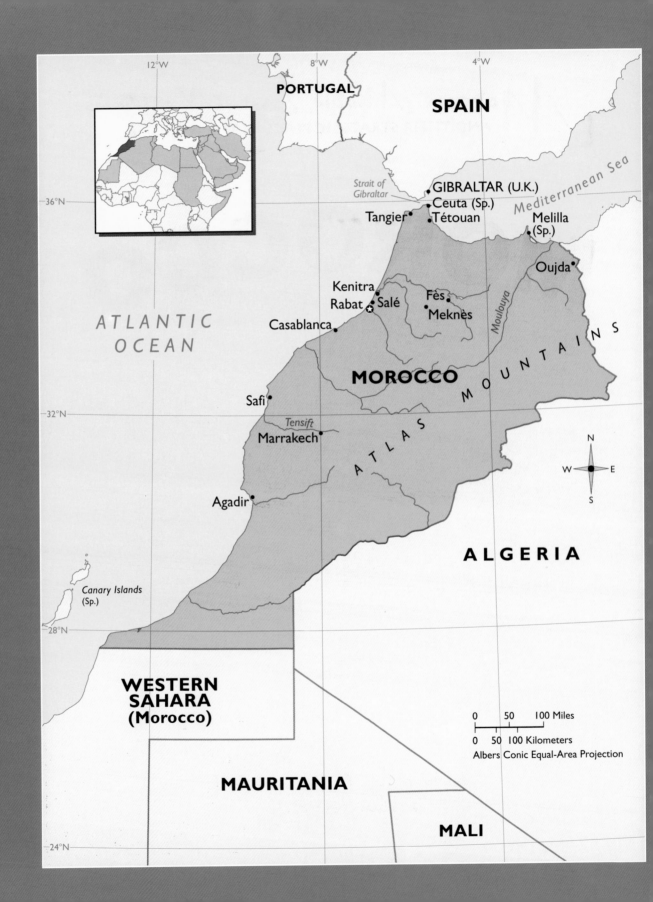

Modern Middle East Nations
AND THEIR STRATEGIC PLACE IN THE WORLD

MOROCCO

LYNDA COHEN CASSANOS

MASON CREST PUBLISHERS
PHILADELPHIA

Produced by OTTN Publishing, Stockton, New Jersey

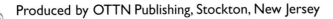
Mason Crest Publishers
370 Reed Road
Broomall, PA 19008
www.masoncrest.com

First printing

1 3 5 7 9 8 6 4 2

Library of Congress Cataloging-in-Publication Data

Cassanos, Lynda Cohen.
  Morocco / Lynda Cohen Cassanos.
      p. cm. — (Modern Middle East nations and their strategic
place in the world)
Summary: Discusses the geography, history, economy, government,
religion, people, foreign relations, and major cities of Morocco.
Includes bibliographical references and index.
  ISBN 1-59084-515-3
1. Morocco—Juvenile literature. [1. Morocco.] I. Title. II. Series.
DT305 .C265 2003
964—dc21

                                        2002013006

Modern Middle East Nations
AND THEIR STRATEGIC PLACE IN THE WORLD

TABLE OF CONTENTS

Modern Middle East Nations

AND THEIR STRATEGIC PLACE IN THE WORLD

ALGERIA
BAHRAIN
DJIBOUTI
EGYPT
IRAN
IRAQ
ISRAEL
JORDAN
KUWAIT
LEBANON
LIBYA
MAURITANIA
THE MIDDLE EAST: FACTS AND FIGURES
MOROCCO
OMAN
THE PALESTINIANS
QATAR
SAUDI ARABIA
SOMALIA
SUDAN
SYRIA
TUNISIA
TURKEY
UNITED ARAB EMIRATES
YEMEN

Dr. Harvey Sicherman, president and director of the Foreign Policy Research Institute, is the author of such books as *America the Vulnerable: Our Military Problems and How to Fix Them* (2002) and *Palestinian Autonomy, Self-Government and Peace* (1993).

Introduction

by Dr. Harvey Sicherman

Situated as it is between Africa, Europe, and the Far East, the Middle East has played a unique role in world history. Often described as the birthplace of religions (notably Judaism, Christianity, and Islam) and the cradle of civilizations (Egypt, Mesopotamia, Persia), this region and its peoples have given humanity some of its most precious possessions. At the same time, the Middle East has had more than its share of conflicts. The area is strewn with the ruins of fortifications and the cemeteries of combatants, not to speak of modern arsenals for war.

Today, more than ever, Americans are aware that events in the Middle East can affect our security and prosperity. The United States has a considerable military, political, and economic presence throughout much of the region. Developments there regularly find their way onto the front pages of our newspapers and the screens of our television sets.

Still, it is fair to say that most Middle Eastern countries remain a mystery, their cultures and religions barely known, their peoples and politics confusing and strange. The purpose of this book series is to change that, to educate the reader in the basic facts about the 23 states and many peoples that make up the region. (For our purpose, the Middle East also includes the North African states linked by ethnicity, language, and religion to the Arabs, as well as Somalia and Mauritania, which are African but share the Muslim religion and are members of the Arab League.) A notable feature of the series is the integration of geography, demography, and history; economics and politics; culture and religion. The careful student will learn much that he or she needs to know about ever so important lands.

A few general observations are in order as an introduction to the subject matter.

The first has to do with history and politics. The modern Middle East is full of ancient sites and peoples who trace their lineage and literature to antiquity. Many commentators also attribute the Middle East's political conflicts to grievances and rivalries from the distant past. While history is often invoked, the truth is that the modern Middle East political system dates only from the 1920s and was largely created by the British and the French, the victors of World War I. Such states as Algeria, Iraq, Israel, Jordan, Kuwait, Saudi Arabia, Syria, Turkey, and the United Arab Emirates did not exist before 1914—they became independent between 1920 and 1971. Others, such as Egypt and Iran, were dominated by outside powers until well after World War II. Before 1914, most of the region's states were either controlled by the Turkish-run Ottoman Empire or owed allegiance to the Ottoman sultan. (The sultan was also the caliph or highest religious authority in Islam, in the line of the prophet Muhammad's successors, according to the beliefs of the majority of Muslims known as the Sunni.) It was this imperial Muslim system that was ended by the largely British military victory over the Ottomans in World War I. Few of the leaders who emerged in the wake of this event were happy with the territories they were assigned or the borders, which were often drawn by Europeans. Yet, the system has endured despite many efforts to change it.

The second observation has to do with economics, demography, and natural resources. The Middle Eastern peoples live in a region of often dramatic geographical contrasts: vast parched deserts and high mountains, some with year-round snow; stone-hard volcanic rifts and lush semi-tropical valleys; extremely dry and extremely wet conditions, sometimes separated by only a few miles; large permanent rivers and *wadis*, riverbeds dry as a bone until winter rains send torrents of flood from the mountains to the sea. In ancient times, a very skilled agriculture made the Middle East the breadbasket of the Roman Empire, and its trade carried luxury fabrics, foods, and spices both East and West.

Most recently, however, the Middle East has become more known for a single commodity—oil, which is unevenly distributed and largely concentrated in the Persian Gulf and Arabian Peninsula (although large pockets are also to be found in Algeria, Libya, and other sites). There are also new, potentially lucrative offshore gas fields in the Eastern Mediterranean.

This uneven distribution of wealth has been compounded by demographics. Birth rates are very high, but the countries with the most oil are often lightly populated. Over the last decade, Middle East populations under the age of 20 have grown enormously. How will these young people be educated? Where will they work? The failure of most governments in the region to give their people skills and jobs (with notable exceptions such as Israel) has also contributed to large out-migrations. Many have gone to Europe; many others work in other Middle Eastern countries, supporting their families from afar.

Another unsettling situation is the heavy pressure both people and industry have put on vital resources. Chronic water shortages plague the region. Air quality, public sanitation, and health services in the big cities are also seriously overburdened. There are solutions to these problems, but they require a cooperative approach that is sorely lacking.

A third important observation is the role of religion in the Middle East. Americans, who take separation of church and state for granted, should know that most countries in the region either proclaim their countries to be Muslim or allow a very large role for that religion in public life. Among those with predominantly Muslim populations, Turkey alone describes itself as secular and prohibits avowedly religious parties in the political system. Lebanon was a Christian-dominated state, and Israel continues to be a Jewish state. While both strongly emphasize secular politics, religion plays an enormous role in culture, daily life, and legislation. It is also important to recall that Islamic law (*Shariah*) permits people to practice Judaism and Christianity in Muslim states but only as *Dhimmi*, protected but very second-class citizens.

Fourth, the American student of the modern Middle East will be impressed by the varieties of one-man, centralized rule, very unlike the workings of Western democracies. There are monarchies, some with traditional methods of consultation for tribal elders and even ordinary citizens, in Saudi Arabia and many Gulf States; kings with limited but still important parliaments (such as in Jordan and

Morocco); and military and civilian dictatorships, some (such as Syria) even operating on the hereditary principle (Hafez al Assad's son Bashar succeeded him). Turkey is a practicing democracy, although a special role is given to the military that limits what any government can do. Israel operates the freest democracy, albeit constricted by emergency regulations (such as military censorship) due to the Arab-Israeli conflict.

In conclusion, the MODERN MIDDLE EAST NATIONS series will engage imagination and interest simply because it covers an area of such great importance to the United States. Americans may be relative latecomers to the affairs of this region, but our involvement there will endure. We at the Foreign Policy Research Institute hope that these books will kindle a lifelong interest in the fascinating and significant Middle East.

The seawall and 15th-century Portuguese fort at Asilah, a picturesque city on the Atlantic coast of Morocco, just south of Tangier.

Place in the World

An old Arab saying proclaims, "Tunisia is a woman, Algeria is a man, and Morocco is a lion." Indeed, the Kingdom of Morocco, located on the northwest coast of Africa, has long had a proud reputation. The region's earliest known inhabitants, the **Berbers**, have kept their own language and cultural identity. Morocco was the only North African state to resist takeover by the powerful Ottoman Turks; in the 20th century, it gained independence from France six years before its neighbor and rival Algeria. Morocco has close ties to the Western nations and was one of the first Muslim countries to condemn the terrorist attacks of September 11, 2001.

TRANSITIONS AND TRADITIONS

Morocco is ruled by a king who serves as both a political and religious leader. Developing rapidly, the country is in the process of transition from a feudal to a modern state. The young king, Mohammed VI, has made changes to streamline the country's bureaucracy and move Morocco toward democracy. But the nation's problems—unemployment, illiteracy, and poverty—are profound and will be difficult to overcome. Pollution harms Morocco's environment and drought has affected its economy. In the Arab world generally, traditions are embraced and reform is resisted. If the king succeeds—while maintaining stability and avoiding the violence that has plagued neighboring Algeria— Morocco should serve as a positive example of modernization for other Arab nations.

For thousands of years Morocco has been a spiritual, artistic, and intellectual center. In ancient times it was a vibrant crossroads for trade from Europe, sub-Saharan Africa, and the East. Caravans carrying gold, silver, and slaves crossed the rough terrain. The early influence of the Phoenicians, Romans, Byzantines, Arabs, and Jews sparked the country's rich cultural development, which then flourished throughout the centuries.

Early Arab geographers called Morocco Al-Maghreb al-Aqsa, "the farthest land of the setting sun." The country is still referred to in Arabic as "the Maghreb." Although this usage is correct, the word *Maghreb* generally means all of North Africa, including Morocco, Algeria, Tunisia, and often Libya.

Modern Morocco is a mix of Middle Eastern, Western, and African cultures. The country is known as the gate to Africa and the bridge to Europe. It is a generally tolerant nation where the spirituality of the Islamic East meets peacefully with the modern culture of the West.

A LAND THAT BECKONS TRAVELERS

This magnificent land has long been a magnet for travelers. Western artists and writers such as the French painters Eugène Delacroix and Henri Matisse and the American novelist Edith

Wharton visited Morocco; their works were influenced by its beautiful scenery and people. In the late 1940s and 1950s writers such as Paul and Jane Bowles, Truman Capote, Tennessee Williams, Allen Ginsberg, and Jack Kerouac reveled in the literary and free-wheeling ambiance of Tangier. Wealthy Europeans and Americans also gravitated to the port city.

To this day, Morocco continues to attract the famous and not so famous to its shores. In Morocco the exotic is reality—the fabled **souks**, **fantasias**, tribal celebrations, and snake charmers still exist. There are desert nomads called "blue men" because their skin is tinted blue from the indigo dye in their robes. Amulets, magical charms, and **henna** tattoos grace the faces, hands, and ankles of many Berber women. In the countryside, religious brotherhoods perform rhythmic, trance-inducing rituals to cure illness.

What is it about Morocco that stirs a fierce attachment on the part of its people and continues to attract visitors from afar? Perhaps what is compelling about this North African country is its ability to preserve the old and delight in the new. A person who enters the **medina** in Fez will find one of the largest, most vital medieval cities in the world. On the boulevards in cosmopolitan Casablanca, visitors will encounter Internet cafés, fast-food franchises, and women in modern dress. Morocco's mobile telephone network serves more than 85 percent of the population, and the country has hundreds of Internet providers. At the same time, approximately 80 percent of the villages still have dirt roads and lack electricity and running water. Morocco, a land of spectacular beaches, windsurfing, golf courses, and skiing, also has a history of human-rights violations and imprisonment of political dissidents. However, as Morocco enters the 21st century, optimism is strong and changes abound. The regal, independent character of the country endures, and the warmth and hospitality of the people remain— still expressed with a welcome glass of hot, sweet mint tea.

A popular spot for tourists is the Cascades d'Ouzoud, where the water falls some 330 feet (100 meters). Morocco's topography is varied and includes moist coastal areas, dry deserts, lush forests, and numerous mountain ranges.

The Land

Morocco, located on the northwest corner of the vast African continent, is the most westerly country in the Arab world. Approximately 8 miles (13 kilometers) from Spain across the Strait of Gibraltar, Morocco is closer to Europe than any other African country. The Strait of Gibraltar is also the demarcation between Morocco's two coasts: east of Gibraltar is the Mediterranean coast; to the west and south is the Atlantic. Because of its strategic location at the crossroads of Europe, Africa, and the Arab world, Morocco has been invaded and colonized numerous times throughout history.

With 172,413 square miles (446,550 sq km) of territory, Morocco is slightly larger than California. The disputed Western Sahara region, much of which Morocco has controlled since 1976, adds 102,703 square miles (266,000 sq km) to the country's total area. Morocco claims 2,175 miles (3,500 km) of coastline, including the Western Sahara; without the disputed desert territory, Morocco's coastline is about half as long, 1,140 miles (1,835 km). Morocco is bordered on the north by the Strait of Gibraltar and the Mediterranean Sea; to the south by Mauritania (south of the Western Sahara); to the west by the Atlantic Ocean; and to the east and southeast by Algeria.

The Spanish **enclaves** of Ceuta and Melilla—legacies of Spain's long involvement in the area—are on Morocco's Mediterranean coast. Ceuta, located on a peninsula just east of Tangier on the northeast tip of Africa, covers about 7 square miles (19 sq km). It has been a Spanish enclave since 1580. Located on another peninsula closer to Algeria, the even smaller Melilla has been a Spanish enclave since 1497. Spain also owns the Chafarinas, five small islands off Morocco's Mediterranean coast that have been used as Spanish military bases and prisons, as well as the larger Canary

A Moroccan village next to an oasis in the shadow of the Atlas Mountains.

This map shows the range of topographic features in Morocco. From a coastal plain the land rises into several mountain ranges, then gradually drops off and becomes the Sahara Desert.

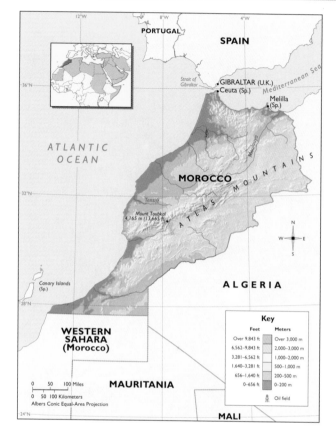

Islands, off the north Atlantic coast of Morocco and the Western Sahara.

Morocco has many natural environments, from sandy beaches and rugged mountains to verdant forests and arid desert. The highest mountains and the most extensive system of rivers in North Africa are found in Morocco. The natural barriers of the Atlas Mountains to the east and the desert to the south separate Morocco both physically and psychologically from the rest of the great African continent. A land rich in contrasts, Morocco's unique geography has nurtured an autonomous spirit and played an important role in shaping the country's development.

Morocco's four mountain ranges—the Rif, the Middle Atlas, the High (or Grand) Atlas, and the Anti Atlas—command the interior region, dividing the temperate coast from the Sahara Desert.

Cliffs on the coast of Morocco drop off into the Atlantic Ocean. Many Moroccans live in cities and communities along the coast.

Morocco has three main geographic regions: the Atlantic coastal lowlands and coastal **plateau**; the mountainous interior, which includes plateaus, plains, and fertile valleys; and the eastern and southern desert region. One-third of Morocco's landscape is mountainous.

COASTAL LOWLANDS

The broad coastal lowlands, called the Taza Depression, extend south along the Atlantic coast, from Tangier to Essaouira. Many of Morocco's large cities are located in this zone, including Kenitra,

Rabat, Casablanca, Mohammedia, and Safi. The low, flat Atlantic coast, covered with sand dunes and marshes, has few natural harbors.

The land slowly rises from the Atlantic to form a large, open, irregular plateau that covers thousands of square miles. The plateau sits at elevations between 1,770 and 2,950 feet (540 and 900 meters) before giving way to mountains. The soil is poor, but some areas on the plateau contain rich phosphate deposits that contribute to Morocco's role as one of the world's largest producers of this mineral.

Two plains in this area have especially good soil for farming: the Tadla Plain, located on the Oum er Rhia River, which is covered in a rich deposit of silt; and the Haouz, at the basin of the Tensift River near Marrakech (also spelled Marrakesh). But the richest agricultural regions in the country are three other plains on the plateau: the Gharb, Chaouia, and Souss Plains. Located between the Atlantic coast and the High and Middle Atlas Mountains, they receive moderate rainfall and are irrigated by water from numerous shallow rivers.

MOUNTAINS

Past the plains and plateaus lie the mountain ranges. The most northerly range is the Rif. The Rif Mountains curve in an arc from the Strait of Gibraltar east to the hills of Aith Said. These limestone and sandstone peaks seldom exceed heights of 7,220 feet (2,200 meters). The highest point is Mount Tidirhine, at just over 8,000 feet (2,450 meters). Erosion has sculpted deep ravines in the Rif, especially on the north-facing, seaward side. These almost impenetrable mountains, which isolate northern Morocco from the rest of the country, run parallel to the Mediterranean Sea. One natural pass, called the Taza Gap, provides access from the Atlantic through the Rif and the Middle Atlas Mountains; it is the only access route between the ocean and the rest of North Africa. The severe Rif chain, 180 miles (290 km) long, and the rugged Mediterranean coastline form, in the words of writer Marvin W. Mikesell, "a secluded mountain region, difficult of access, which at all times enabled its Berber inhabitants to keep their necks free of foreign yoke."

To the south of the Rif, the Atlas mountain chain crosses the middle of Morocco from the southwest to the northeast. The Atlas Mountains separate the Atlantic plains from the rest of North Africa. They contain numerous mineral deposits that include lead, zinc, iron, manganese, and phosphates; they also contain gold and silver. There are very few passes through these harsh mountains. The chain is actually three separate mountain ranges: the Middle Atlas (Moyen Atlas), in the northeast; the High Atlas (Haut Atlas), in the central area; and the Anti Atlas, in the southwest. At certain points the ranges overlap each other on a northeast-southwest axis. The entire range extends approximately 1,500 miles (2,414 km).

The Middle Atlas Mountains, separated from the Rif by the Taza Gap, reach a height of about 10,960 feet (3,340 meters). Oil exploration has taken place on the plateaus of these mountains, and they are a major watershed, dependent upon rain and melting snow. The Sebou River, which rises south of Fez (also spelled Fès), and the Umm er-Rbia River, which begins northeast of Khenifra, flow through the Middle Atlas range to the Atlantic Ocean. The Sebou River, combined with its tributaries, represents 45 percent of the country's water resources. The Moulouya River is the only major river that flows into the Mediterranean Sea. Morocco's rivers, too shallow for navigation, are used for irrigation and electric power. The northern end of the Middle Atlas was an important trans-Saharan trade route, extending south to Tafilalt and across the Sahara.

The High Atlas range is, for the most part, parallel to the southern area of the Middle Atlas. Snow-covered in winter and spring, the High Atlas Mountains are the tallest range in the country and contain Morocco's highest peak, Jebel Toubkal, at 13,665 feet (4,165 meters). Two rivers flow from the High Atlas to the Sahara: the Drâa—at 746 miles (1,200 km) Morocco's longest river—and the Ziz. Occasionally, the Drâa will follow its entire course as far as the Atlantic coast, north of Tan Tan, but most often part of it is dry. The Tensift, another major river in the range, flows in a westerly direction and is about 168 miles (270 km) in length. The High and

The Geography of Morocco

Location: northern Africa, bordering the North Atlantic Ocean and the Mediterranean Sea, between Algeria and Western Sahara

Area: slightly larger than California
  total: 172,413 square miles (446,550 sq km)
  land: 172,316 square miles (446,300 sq km)
  water: 97 square miles (250 sq km)

Borders: Algeria, 969 miles (1,559 km); Western Sahara, 275 miles (443 km); Spain, 9.9 miles (15.9 km)—Ceuta: 3.9 miles (6.3 km); Melilla: 6 miles (9.6 km)

Climate: Mediterranean, becoming more extreme in the interior

Terrain: extensive plateaus, valleys, and rich lowland coastal plains border mountainous northern coast and interior; Western Sahara desert is mainly low and flat; the sandy, rocky terrain rises into small mountains in the northeast and south

Elevation extremes:
  lowest point: Sebkha Tah, 180 feet (55 meters) below sea level
  highest point: Jebel Toubkal, 13,665 feet (4,165 meters)

Natural hazards: northern mountains geologically unstable and subject to earthquakes; periodic droughts

Source: Adapted from CIA World Factbook, 2001.

Middle Atlas Mountains support luxuriant forests of cedar, cork, oak, and pine trees, particularly on their northern sides. In contrast, the southern slopes are more arid, with rocky areas and sparse vegetation. The southern valleys of the High Atlas, including the famous Drâa and Dades Valleys, feature spectacular landscapes.

The Anti Atlas Mountains, the most southerly range, are separated from the High Atlas in the west by the agricultural valley of the Sous River. They are the lowest of the four mountain chains, though the 8,304-foot (2,531-meter) peak Jebel Aklim is found here. To the east of the Drâa River, the Anti Atlas Mountains resemble a high, arid plateau, and the range becomes a massif of old rocks that reach elevations of about 7,875 feet (2,400 meters). To the east and south the mountains become rocky and descend gradually into the Sahara Desert.

DESERT

The third main geographic region of Morocco, the desert, covers the area south of Agadir on the west coast to Figuig in the east. This boundary marks the beginning of the Sahara Desert, a barren region of sand dunes, rocks, stones, and scattered **oases**. Sebkha Tah, the lowest point in the country, lies south of Tarfaya, just at the Western Sahara. It is 180 feet (55 meters) below sea level. Combined with the Western Sahara, one-half of Morocco is desert. By comparison, 90 percent of Algeria and two-thirds of Tunisia—the two nations to the east of Morocco—are composed of desert.

The contested Western Sahara borders the Atlantic Ocean between Mauritania and Morocco. Approximately the size of Colorado, it is a low, flat desert area with expanses of small rocky or sandy mountains in the south and northeast. Rain is unusual in this intensely hot region, though cold offshore air currents create fog and heavy dew, and a dusty haze often covers the land.

A camel makes its way across Saharan dunes. Camels were domesticated thousands of years ago by Arab traders, and they soon became a primary source of transport for desert-dwellers.

CLIMATE

Along its coastal areas Morocco enjoys a Mediterranean climate, though the Atlantic coast is not as warm as the Mediterranean coast because of the effects of the cool Canary Current. The average temperature in Tangier and Casablanca ranges from 54ºF (12ºC) in the winter to 77ºF (25ºC) and higher in the summer.

The weather in the interior is more extreme. In the summer, temperatures in Marrakech may exceed 104ºF (40ºC). When the *sirocco*, a hot dry wind from the Sahara, blows across the region, temperatures rise even more. In the winter, the interior is still hot, with daytime temperatures averaging around 86ºF (30ºC), but the nights are very cool. The oases, torrid by day, can dip below freezing during winter nights. In this compact country, one may experience the dry heat of the Sahara and the humid, snowy heights of the Atlas Mountains all in one day's travel.

There are two distinct seasons in Morocco: the rainy season, in winter and spring; and the dry season, in summer and early fall. The rainy season usually runs from October or November to April or May. The country experiences almost all of its annual rainfall during this period. In Marrakech, yearly rainfall averages 9 inches (23 centimeters); in Rabat, 21 inches (53 cm). The Rif and the northern Middle Atlas experience the most rainfall, although summers are dry. During the dry season, which runs from May or June to September or October, serious droughts may occur.

NATURAL AND MAN-MADE HAZARDS

Geologically, northern Morocco is unstable, and the country is susceptible to earthquakes. The last major earthquake, in 1960, struck Agadir, on the Atlantic coast. Approximately 12,000 people were killed in this natural disaster.

The country is also prone to droughts. Over the past century, a drought has hit Morocco about one year out of three.

Morocco faces many of the same environmental problems that exist throughout the developing world. Rapid population growth, urbanization, and an absence of strict industrial regulations have led to environmental degradation in Morocco, as well as in neighboring Algeria and Tunisia. As a result of better health care, sanitation, food resources, and security in the 20th century, Morocco's population increased from 5.8 million in 1921 to about 30 million in 2001. By 2025 it is projected to exceed 45 million.

An oasis—a fertile area in the desert where water can be found—at Tafraout. In the desert areas of Morocco, communities grew up around oases such as this. A village of Ammeln Berbers thrives near the Tafraout oasis.

More than half of Morocco's people live in urban centers, where most industry is also located. In these cities, water supplies are often contaminated by raw sewage, and factory emissions frequently make the air unhealthful. In rural areas overgrazing, drought, and the excessive clearing of wooded areas for construction materials, fuel, and fodder have allowed the desert to expand. Annually, the country loses in excess of 61,000 acres (about 25,000 hectares) of forest, which results in widespread soil erosion and thus a reduction of crop yield. Approximately one-third of Morocco's ecosystems are damaged. The government and international organizations such as the Peace Corps and the United Nations have begun to focus on Morocco's environmental problems, but the situation remains serious.

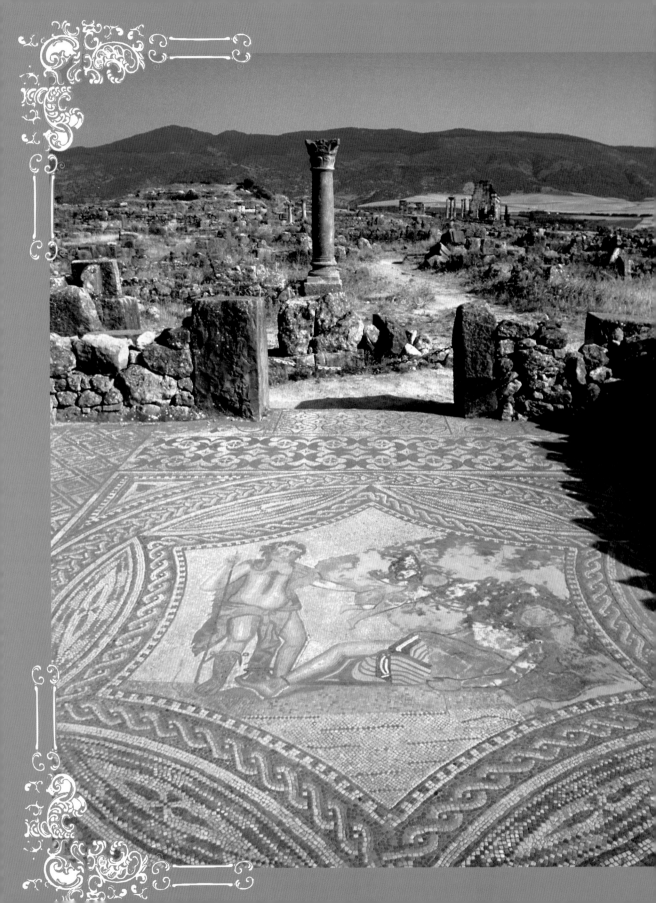

These Roman remains in Volubilis include an ornate mosaic floor. Morocco's long history has seen periods of rule by Europeans, including the Romans more than 2,000 years ago, the Portuguese and Spanish in the 16th and 17th centuries, and, more recently, the French.

History

The human history of Morocco begins in the Middle Paleolithic period, from 80,000 to 35,000 B.C. North Africa was then a vast savannah, or grassland, and joining the elephants, ostriches, and giraffes of the region was Neanderthal man. From 5,000 to 2,000 B.C. the Sahara region dried up and became a natural barrier between what was to become Morocco and the south. To escape drought, the people of the Sahara fled first to the Atlas Mountains, and then to the coast. Migrants from the Mediterranean and southwest Asia joined them, thus planting the roots of Berber civilization. Cave paintings by inhabitants of these early communities still exist in the Anti Atlas Mountains.

Around 1200 B.C. the Phoenicians ventured from their home in the eastern Mediterranean. A maritime people, they did not conquer or colonize. Instead, they established trading posts and fish-salting factories along the Mediterranean

Prehistoric sandstone carvings such as this can be seen near Oukaimeden in the High Atlas Mountains of Morocco.

coast of North Africa, including Morocco. The Phoenicians ignored the **_indigenous_** tribes and poor agricultural lands to the south.

ROMAN INFLUENCE

One of the early Phoenician settlements in North Africa grew to become Carthage, located in what is now Tunisia. The Carthaginians colonized Morocco's northern coast in the fifth century B.C. Unlike the Phoenicians, the Carthaginians grew wheat, introduced the grape, and exported anchovy paste. The north coast settlements became prosperous towns as fish salting and preserving grew into a major industry. During this period, the indigenous inland tribes, called Mauri, established an informal confederation that they called Mauritania.

Meanwhile, Carthage and Rome fought for supremacy in the western Mediterranean, engaging in a series of three wars known as the Punic Wars. After the Romans conquered Carthage in 146 B.C., during the Third Punic War, many Carthaginians fled west, to what is now Morocco and Algeria, to escape slavery. The victorious Romans soon followed. When they arrived, the fierce Mauri, whom the Romans labeled barbarians, or Berbers, confronted them. The Berbers fought the Romans for more than 100 years, but the invaders were able to establish the colonies of Salé, Colonia, Lixus, and Volubilis. A Berber-Roman civilization began to flourish. The Roman emperor Octavius granted the Kingdom of Mauritania to Juba II, a young Berber prince, and eventually added Numidia (Algeria) to his realm. Juba II, a wise ruler educated in Rome, was married to Selene, the daughter of Mark Antony and Cleopatra. He reigned from 25 B.C. to A.D. 23.

In A.D. 40, the Roman emperor Caligula assassinated Ptolemy, Juba II's son. The Mauritanians revolted against the Romans but were defeated. Mauritania, which included most of Morocco at this time, became the Roman province of Mauritania Tingitania.

The remainder of the Roman era became a period of darkness and stagnation for Morocco. The Berbers' lives remained unchanged except in the isolated Roman colonies, where there was a mixed cultural heritage. As Rome declined, Germanic tribes called Vandals and Goths plundered modern-day Spain and Italy. In 429 the Vandal chief Genseric and his army invaded Morocco. After the fall of the Roman Empire, in the late fifth century, most of Morocco returned to its tribal, clan-dominated existence.

THE COMING OF ISLAM

Islam, a religion born in the Arabian Peninsula, began to spread rapidly following the death of its founder, the prophet Muhammad, in 632. Within a few decades, conquering Arab Islamic armies had reached Morocco. During this period of Arab conquest, many Berbers became Muslims, as believers in Islam are called. But many Berbers also resisted the conquerors.

In 681 Oqba ben Nafi, the great Muslim hero of the conquest of North Africa, led his troops in a legendary (and perhaps purely mythical) march to the Atlantic Ocean. Between 705 and 709 Moussa ibn Noceir, the Muslim Umayyad dynasty's new governor of North Africa, brought the area of present-day Morocco under Arab rule. He left his client, Tariq bin Zayyad, a Berber, in charge of Tangier. In 711 Tariq commanded the Berber and Arab troops that crossed into Spain, beginning more than seven centuries of Islamic influence in that European country. His name was given to Jabal Tariq, the Rock of Gibraltar.

THE DYNASTIC PERIOD

Although many Berbers had by this time converted to Islam, instability in Morocco continued until 788. In that year Idriss ben Abdallah arrived in Volubilis. A *sharif*, or descendant of the prophet Muhammad through Muhammad's daughter Fatima, Idriss was revered by the Berbers for his pious, learned manner. The Berber chiefs proclaimed him their king, and he married a Berber princess named Lalla Kenza, thus symbolically uniting Berber and Arab cultures. During his reign the country's leaders became known as *sultans*, and Morocco's first dynasty, the Idrissid dynasty, began. The Idrissids would rule for nearly 300 years, from 788 to 1055.

Idriss ben Abdallah's 12-year-old son, Idriss II, became sultan in 809. Under Idriss II many tribes converted to Islam and new regions were added to his realm. Fez, founded in 789, became the capital city and a major religious and cultural center for the Islamic world. In 818, about 8,000 Muslim immigrants, expelled by the Christians from Córdoba, Spain, settled in Fez. Two thousand families also arrived from Kairouan, Tunisia. These new residents brought skills and resources that enhanced the spiritual and intellectual life of

Ait Benhaddou is a traditional Berber walled village; the buildings and walls are made from mud bricks. Islamic Berber dynasties ruled Morocco for hundreds of years.

the capital.

The Idrissid dynasty collapsed by 1055 when the Almoravids conquered Sijilmassa, the center of caravan and trans-Sahara trade. From this point to the mid-1400s, Morocco's dynastic families evolved from three main Berber tribes: the Sanhaja, the Masmoda, and the Zenata. The Almoravids, members of the Sanhaja tribe, were camel-riding nomads from the western Sahara, on a quest to conquer the Maghreb and restore Islam to what they viewed as its true form. They founded the city of Marrakech in 1062 and made it their capital. Violent and successful, the Almoravids conquered much of the desert and the south for Islam, as well as parts of Spain, including Valencia. Their dynasty lasted from 1055 to about 1147.

Eventually their vast Spanish-Moroccan empire declined as the Spanish Christians became more powerful and the tribes in the Atlas rebelled. The next rulers, the Almohad (in power from 1130 to 1269), came from the Masmoda tribe; these people were farmers from the High Atlas Mountains. Marrakech remained their capital, Fez blossomed, and, by the end of the 12th century, Morocco had reached a high point of artistic and intellectual growth. By the mid-13th century, however, battles for succession, apathetic leaders, and the loss of control of the Saharan trade routes led to the fall of the Almohads.

In 1269 the Beni Marin, a rugged, horseback-riding tribe of Zenata Berbers from the harsh interior, began the Marinid dynasty (1269–1465) with the capture of Marrakech. Abor Youssef Yacoub, the dynasty's first sultan, promoted orthodox Islam and ***jihad***, or holy war. He defended persecuted Spanish Muslims, slowed the spread of Christianity in southern Spain, and saved the city of Granada from Spanish conquest. The Marinids made Fez their capital.

The third Marinid ruler, Abou el-Hassan—called the Black Sultan because his mother was Abyssinian—revived a Berber empire that extended from Tunis to the Atlantic. The most capable of the dynasty's leaders, he built ***madrassas***—colleges for Muslim learning—in Fez; these also became the first centers of Hispano-Moorish art. (*Moorish* refers to the Arab-Berber conquerors of Spain, or simply to the Berbers.) The original *mellahs*, neighborhoods that segregated and protected the Jewish population, were created in 1438, and a simple form of civil service was begun.

During the 15th century, however, the Marinid dynasty declined. It lost Algeria and Tunisia, while the Christians advanced steadily in Granada. The Spanish moved toward Morocco in 1415,

This decorated page from a Moroccan copy of the Qur'an dates from the 12th century. It was produced during Almohad rule over Morocco. Islam has been the dominant religion of the region since the 7th century.

the Portuguese invaded Ceuta on the northern coast, and the Ottoman Turks entered Tlemcen, in the east. Ibn Wattis, the new sovereign, signed a treaty with Portugal that allowed the Portuguese to control most of the western coast.

Under the Wattasid dynasty (1465–1549), the country continued to suffer European assaults, internal fighting, and political and economic decline. Portugal seized land on Morocco's coasts, resulting in widespread warfare between Muslims and Christians in the western Mediterranean. An Islamic revival and call for jihad began in Morocco in response to the difficult times. Muslim **corsairs**, or sea raiders who commanded private warships, were licensed by the ruling authorities to attack Christian vessels. Moroccans built the port of Salé as a base for corsairs—who were referred to by the Europeans as the Barbary pirates.

The Sa'adians (1525–1659), from the Souss region, were granted sovereignty by the Wattasids. They established the next powerful dynasty, centered in Marrakech, and managed a successful jihad against the Christians. The Sa'adians were *shurafa* (the plural form of *sharif*—that is, Arabic descendants of the prophet Muhammad through Fatima and Ali). Under their sultan, Mohammed al-Cheikh, they expelled the Christians from Agadir, Safi, and Azemmour. But Christian Europe and the Muslim Ottoman Empire were still threats. The sultan formed an unanticipated alliance with Spain that ended Ottoman expansion in Morocco. In 1578 King Sebastian of Portugal attacked Morocco. In the battle that followed, the Portuguese army was defeated, King Sebastian was killed, numerous Portuguese trading posts were closed, and Portuguese expansion in Morocco ended.

The peaceful interlude that followed was short-lived. The Sa'adians' once wealthy, vibrant empire collapsed in anarchy and corruption at the beginning of the 17th century. After more than 50 years of civil war, in 1659 the sharifian Alawite family took over the government left vacant by the Sa'adians. The Alawite family rules to this day.

The remains of an English castle in Tangier face the Mediterranean Sea. The city was given to the English ruler, King Charles II, as part of the dowry of Catherine of Braganza, a Portuguese princess whom he married in 1662. Tangier was held by the English until 1684, when they decided to abandon the city because of the high cost of defending it.

The Alawite dynasty was led first by **Moulay** Rachid (1664–1672), and then by Rachid's brother, Moulay Ismail (1672–1727), one of the most renowned sultans of Morocco. Moulay Ismail, famous for his love of grandeur, moved the capital to Meknès, where he constructed enormous buildings and numerous fortresses. He cultivated diplomatic relations with France's "Sun King," Louis XIV, and tried, unsuccessfully, to marry the king's daughter. The sultan recaptured the towns of Larache and Tangier from the Europeans, and raised an army of 150,000 men, consisting mostly of Abids, descendants of slaves brought to Morocco by the Sa'adians. When Moulay Ismail died, his army, left without a leader, was responsible for much of the chaos that followed.

During the 18th century, most European powers signed treaties with the Moroccan sultans, and the country's corsair fleet was reduced. In 1769 the Alawite ruler **Sidi** Mohammed ben Abdallah (1757–1790) developed the Atlantic port city of Essaouira. In 1777 Sidi Mohammed became the first head of state to recognize American independence, and in 1786 America and Morocco signed the first treaty between the United States and an African or Arab nation.

ECONOMIC WEAKNESS AND POLITICAL INSTABILITY

Morocco entered the 19th century as an economically weak and unstable country. As Europe welcomed the industrial revolution and democratic freedom, Morocco remained mired in its medieval past. Moroccans had little knowledge of the European people to the north, and the mountains separated them from Muslims to the east. When 18th-century Moroccan ambassadors described their travels across the Strait of Gibraltar, they did not try to differentiate between the various European cultures. They were impressed by the hospitals and military, but were appalled by the public dancing between men and women and the rituals of Christianity. Only a privileged few Moroccans had ever been exposed to foreigners, however.

In 1827 a war between the French and the Ottoman province of Algiers served as a wake-up call for the Moroccan population. On July 5, 1830, the Ottoman dey (governor) in Algeria surrendered and Algeria became a French colony. Because Morocco supported the Algerian resistance, the French forces bombarded Tangier and Essaouira as punishment in 1844. The same year, 30,000 Moroccans were defeated by 11,000 French troops at the Battle of Isly, near the Algerian border. The result was the Treaty of Tangier, which established a definite border between Morocco and Algeria, returned the eastern town of Oujda to Morocco, and required the sultan to end his support of the Algerian resistance.

In 1860 Spain invaded Tetouan, resulting in the Tetouan Agreement, which obligated Morocco to pay large sums to Spain. Morocco was forced to borrow money at high interest rates from Britain. European imperialism was on the rise and Morocco was facing economic ruin.

Sultan Moulay Hassan I (1873–1894) attempted to reform the government and army, but European powers prohibited changes that threatened their interests in the region. By the early 1900s, France and Spain, through military victories and treaties, managed much of the country's economy and government. In 1906, in Algeciras, Spain, 30 international powers met to determine the extent of Europe's influence in Morocco. The resulting treaty, the Act of Algeciras, was signed by 11 European delegations, the United States delegation, and Morocco. The treaty declared "order, peace and prosperity" in Morocco and granted the sultan sovereignty over his people and a land free of European domination.

In reality, Moroccan autonomy was an illusion. The French controlled the new state bank that issued currency, made loans, and acted as the treasury. On June 18, 1906, Moulay Abdelaziz

(1894–1908), a kindly but weak and uneducated sultan, ratified an act that ended his power to make government policy.

The Act of Algeciras angered many Moroccans because it reinforced French military and police control, and the French prospered while the local population remained poor. In 1905 locusts destroyed the crops; the following year the country suffered a drought, and by 1907 starvation was widespread. Riots, attacks on Europeans, and civil disorder prevailed. Moulay Abdelaziz's government collapsed and several powerful tribes demanded that his brother, Moulay Abdelhafid, claim the sultanate. On August 6, 1907, Abdelhafid seized control.

Moroccan hostility toward foreigners grew as the European population increased, the French acquired more land and money, and the Spanish attempted to conquer the Rif. Sultan Abdelhafid was powerless. His attempt to raise extra taxes led to rebellion, as most taxes already went to the French. The hopes of those who brought him to power vanished as Abdelhafid's politics ultimately mirrored his brother's.

FRENCH PROTECTORATE

On May 21, 1911, under the guise of subduing a civil war, French troops occupied Fez. Soon after, the Fez Convention formally established Morocco as a French protectorate, and Moulay Abdelhafid signed the Treaty of Fez, relinquishing his right to govern. While France controlled most of Morocco, Spain was granted the northern zone and the desert regions of the south.

Morocco was administered by a French resident general, Louis-Hubert-Gonzales Lyautey, who held the post from 1912 to 1925. Lyautey, a distinguished officer, believed that the French should work to modernize the country yet respect pre-colonial customs and identity. Ultimately, his liberal ideals clashed with the reality of French control.

Representatives of France and Spain sign a 1912 treaty in Morocco. Under the terms of the Treaty of Fez, Morocco became a French protectorate; Spain was given control of the Rif Mountain area between its coastal enclaves at Melilla and Ceuta.

After the Fez uprising, Sultan Abdelhafid **abdicated**. He was unwilling to be a mere figurehead. Resident General Lyautey chose Abdelhafid's brother, Moulay Youssef—a pleasant but passive man—to succeed him. During Moulay Youssef's sultanate, from 1912 to 1927, the powerful French protectorate was now securely hidden behind the veil of a local ruler who gave the foreigners his complete support.

Lyautey restored the peace; modernized the educational, legal, and administrative systems; and developed the port cities of Casablanca and Kenitra. He built the new areas of Rabat, Fez, and Meknès while preserving their ancient medinas. But angry tribes continued to rebel against European domination.

In 1919 a revolutionary leader named Abd al-Karim led a successful rebellion in the Spanish-held Rif. By 1922 his army controlled the northern mountains, and by 1924 he had declared himself emir, or commander, of the Rif.

On April 12, 1925, Abd al-Karim's troops attacked the French front line. By June 5 they had advanced to within 25 miles (40 km) of Fez. On May 8, 1926, however, an attack by 123,000 French and Spanish troops ended Rifi resistance. Abd al-Karim surrendered to the French on May 26 and was exiled to the island of Réunion in the Indian Ocean.

World War II and its Aftermath

Eighteen-year-old Mohammed V (1909–1961), Moulay Youssef's son, became sultan in 1927. At the outbreak of World War II in 1939, he declared his nation's complete solidarity with the French. Influenced by their sultan, many Moroccans enlisted in the French army. By 1940, when France surrendered to Germany, 47,000 Moroccans had joined the French army, more than 2,000 had been killed, and 18,000 had been imprisoned. Allied troops landed on the Moroccan coast on November 8, 1942, to help protect the country from a German invasion.

After the war, nationalist sentiment intensified. Moroccans had fought side by side with the French in World War II. They believed they were entitled to self-determination. The newly created Istiqlal (Independence) Party grew in popularity. The party's **manifesto**, presented on January 11, 1944, demanded freedom and independence for Morocco under Sidi Mohammed V.

The French rejected the manifesto and arrested Istiqlal leaders. But the demands had popular support. Moroccans boycotted French products; rioting erupted in Salé, Rabat, Casablanca, and Fez; and attacks against the French intensified. Mohammed V asked for self-government and for the return of Moroccan territory controlled by France and Spain. The request was denied and more riots erupted.

In 1953 the French resident general, Augustin-Leon Guillaume, and his right-wing supporters moved to dethrone the sultan for his pro-nationalist leanings. They enlisted the help of the extremist religious brotherhoods in the eastern part of the country, which declared that the sultan was irreligious and not a true representative of Islam. They planned to replace the sultan with the unknown Ben Arafa, a grandson of Sidi Mohammed IV. When word of the plan spread, widespread riots erupted throughout Morocco. Guillaume, claiming that the riots were beyond control, received permission from the French cabinet to remove the sultan. But Sidi Mohammed refused to abdicate. On August 20, 1953, he and his two sons were taken from the palace at gunpoint and exiled to the island of Madagascar in the Indian Ocean. Two years of popular revolt followed. Terrorism, acts of sabotage, and riots expressed Moroccan anger over the loss of their beloved sultan.

Finally the French protectorate began to weaken. On November 16, 1955, Sidi Mohammed returned to a jubilant homeland. On March 2, 1956, the French protectorate officially ended and Morocco became independent. Soon after, Spain left the north, but held on to the enclaves of Ceuta, Melilla, and Sidi Ifni. Tangier, which had become an international city in 1923, was reunited with Morocco. The question of boundaries in the Sahara Desert, however, remained unresolved.

THE CHALLENGES OF INDEPENDENCE

Although obtaining independence was a great achievement, Morocco was confronted with a new set of challenges. No plan had been created for governing post-colonial Morocco. Sidi Mohammed—who now assumed the title of king rather than sultan—faced many internal and external problems, such as power

Moulay Hassan II, king of Morocco, in his office in late 1961. King Hassan took power during a turbulent period in Morocco's history—after the death of his popular father and before the government of the newly independent country was fully formed. He ruled Morocco until 1999.

struggles between the labor unions, the left-wing nationalists, and the more moderate Istiqlal Party. Economic strategy was uncertain. War against French rule still raged in neighboring Algeria, the Cold War between the United States and the Soviet Union was at its high point, and tensions between the Arab nations and the newly established country of Israel further complicated matters. The charismatic Sidi Mohammed had to balance his role as mediator and modernizer with that of a devout Muslim and "Commander of the Faithful."

On February 29, 1960, a major earthquake killed approximately 12,000 people in Agadir and destroyed three-fourths of the port city. Almost a year later, on February 26, the king died during minor surgery, sending more shockwaves through the country.

Mohammed V's 31-year-old son, Hassan II, assumed power as both king and prime minister. Thus he maintained control over almost all aspects of the government, including the military and the police.

Morocco's first constitution was proclaimed on November 18, 1962. Hassan II was now the sovereign ruler over a constitutional monarchy and a multi-party system. In 1963, six months after parliamentary elections were held, Hassan resigned as prime minister. However, when student and worker riots broke out in Casablanca, the king declared a state of emergency, dissolved the parliament, suspended the constitution, and reclaimed the title of prime minister. Morocco had gained its independence, but true modernization was still far away.

Hassan lifted the state of emergency in 1970 and introduced a revised, more liberal constitution in 1972. But Hassan's powerful government was known to stifle free speech and ignore human rights. Corruption and political discontent marred his reign. There were two unsuccessful military coups against the king in 1971 and 1972.

Aware of the need for a unifying goal to rally the country and

King Mohammed VI of Morocco and his wife, Princess Lalla Salma, at the royal palace in Rabat. The young king has been very popular since taking over the government in 1999. The public celebrations of his marriage broke a Moroccan tradition of keeping royal wives hidden.

strengthen Moroccan identity, Hassan II organized the Green March to the Spanish Sahara, which Spain was preparing to vacate. On November 6, 1975, approximately 350,000 unarmed Moroccans marched south to claim sovereignty over the territory. Morocco eventually occupied nearly all of what is now known as the Western Sahara, although whether the area will remain under Moroccan control or attain independence remains unresolved.

King Hassan II died on July 23, 1999. His son, Mohammed VI (born 1964), continues the long line of sharifian Alawites, whose dynasty has lasted more than 300 years. The young king studied law at Mohammed V University in Rabat and in France at the University of Nice, specializing in Maghreb–European Union relations. A more liberal, reform-minded ruler than his father, Mohammed made one of his first official acts as king the dismissal of Driss Basri, the iron-fisted minister of the interior who was considered the power behind the throne during much of Hassan's 38-year reign.

In a country where 70 percent of the population is under 30, Mohammed VI's focus has been on educating and finding jobs for unemployed urban and rural youth, and on improving conditions for the handicapped. During his first year as king, this popular ruler toured the Rif Mountains, an area known for its rebellious subjects and one his father did not set foot in during his four decades of rule. Thousands of cheering subjects came out to greet the king and shake his hand. Not since his grandfather's time have the Moroccan people expressed such enthusiasm for their ruler.

Though clearly a link in the traditional dynastic chain, Mohammed VI has a modern vision and an accessible approach to government designed to move Morocco in a more representative, democratic direction. He has declared, "It is now time for authority to serve the people"—a statement Moroccans hope presages better times ahead.

A chemical production plant at the port city of Safi, where phosphates are made into fertilizer. Phosphate mining and production is a major component of Morocco's economy.

The Economy, Politics, and Religion

Compared with many other developing countries, Morocco has a fairly diversified economy. In addition to its traditional mainstay of agriculture, Morocco boasts the world's largest phosphate reserves; productive fisheries; mining, tourist, and light manufacturing industries; and a strong, increasingly deregulated telecommunications sector. Inflation is under control, averaging about 2 percent, a rate comparable to that in some industrialized nations.

ECONOMIC OVERVIEW

Over the past decade, however, economic growth in Morocco has been slow. This is largely attributable to the effects of a recurring drought. Agriculture is an important part of Morocco's economy. It employs 40 percent of the workforce and, depending on the harvest, accounts for between 15 and 20 percent of the **gross domestic product (GDP)**. GDP, an important measure of the overall size of a nation's economy, is the total value of goods and services the nation produces in one year. Morocco's GDP in 2001, as calculated by the World Bank, stood at more than $33.7 billion, giving Morocco the world's 55th-largest economy. But economic conditions for Morocco's people lagged considerably: per capita GDP—each citizen's average annual share of the wealth generated by the country's economic activity—stood at just $1,180. That placed Morocco 129th among the world's nations. Nearly one of every five Moroccans lives below the poverty line.

AGRICULTURE

Droughts in 1999 and 2000 had a devastating impact on Morocco's wheat and barley cultivation, which plummeted to more than 70 percent below the five-year average. Only 20 percent of Morocco's land is currently cultivated, and more than 90 percent of the arable land relies on rainfall. But new irrigation systems are being developed that will provide more than 2.5 million acres (over 1 million hectares) with a reliable supply of water, thus increasing the country's agricultural output.

Morocco is one of only a few Arab nations with the ability to grow enough food to feed its own population. In an average year, Morocco produces two-thirds of the primary grains of wheat, barley, and corn needed for the country. Citrus fruits and vegetables are also exported to Europe, along with dates, grapes, and olives. Morocco is expanding its production of commercial crops of cotton, sugarcane, sugar beets, and sunflowers. Newer crops, such as tea, tobacco, and soybeans, are being cultivated as well, and the wine industry is growing. The threat of drought, however, casts a shadow over the country's rich agricultural potential. Droughts, which occur on average every three years, place the cereal-growing

A field of fruit trees in the Souss Plain. Nearly half of Morocco's people are employed in agriculture.

lowlands especially at risk and, in spite of the country's mostly temperate climate, limit agricultural expansion.

COMMERCIAL FISHING AND FORESTRY

The waters off the coast of Morocco contain several productive fishing areas. Especially notable are the waters off the country's west coast in the Canary Current, which are abundant in sardines, bonito, and tuna. Main fishing ports include Agadir, Safi, Essaouira, and Casablanca. An important part of the country's economy, the fishing industry employs about 300,000 people and accounts for more than $600 million in export earnings. The fishing industry, however, lacks the modern fleets and processing plants to make it competitive with its European neighbors. Periodic fishing bans help maintain the country's fisheries and prevent over-fishing. Morocco renewed its fisheries agreement with the European Union in 1999.

Forests cover 20 percent of Morocco's total land area (excluding the Western Sahara). The country meets its own timber needs by harvesting the forests in the Middle and High Atlas. Extensive areas of eucalyptus trees provide the charcoal used for cooking fuel; there are also many cork oak forests. Cork and paper pulp are also exported.

INDUSTRY

Morocco's industrial sector accounts for 33 percent of the nation's GDP. Major industries include phosphate mining, manufacturing, construction, public works, and energy. Including the Western Sahara, Morocco possesses two-thirds of the world's phosphate reserves. Phosphates are an essential ingredient in plant fertilizers and are also used to make phosphoric acid (whose industrial uses include rust-proofing metals). The country mined 24 million metric tons of phosphates and its derivatives in 1999.

Round fuel storage tanks are in the foreground of this photograph of the Samir petrochemical process-ing plant at Mohammedia. The refinery has the capacity to process more than 125,000 barrels of oil a day.

An open cast mine for extracting silver. Other minerals, including phosphates, coal, iron ore, copper, and zinc are also mined in Morocco. Open cast mining is controversial, however, because of the environmental damage the technique causes. In addition to transforming the land by leaving large craters, such as the one pictured here, toxic substances such as cyanide, used in the mining process, can pollute groundwater.

That year, phosphates accounted for 18.5 percent of Morocco's total exports and produced $1.4 billion of export earnings. Morocco also mines coal, iron ore, copper, silver, and zinc.

The export-oriented manufacturing sector produces construction materials, chemicals, textiles, footwear, processed foods, wines, and petroleum. Artisans create many high-quality leather goods, carpets, ceramics, woodwork, and fabrics that are both sold locally and exported.

THE SERVICE SECTOR

Transportation, commerce, administration, and other components of the service sector employ one-third of Morocco's labor force and produce approximately one-half of the GDP. The country has 24 ports; Casablanca, one of the largest ports in Africa, handles almost half of all Moroccan imports and exports. Morocco's well-

Moroccan traders use computers to track the performance of the country's stock market in Casablanca. The Casablanca Stock Exchange, established in 1929, is the third-oldest stock exchange in Africa; it also is the third-largest on the continent.

maintained network of roads, one of the best in Africa, was established during colonial times and has since been expanded. The railway employs more than 13,800 workers and transports people and industrial products on approximately 1,240 miles (2,000 km) of track. Morocco has 11 major airports. The largest, the international Mohammed V, is located 16 miles (25 km) south of Casablanca. Royal Air Maroc, the state-owned airline, flies to Europe, North America, western Africa, and the Middle East.

Tourism is an important part of Morocco's economy. The most popular tourist destinations are Agadir and Marrakech. The country's pleasant climate, excellent beaches, unique architecture, and diverse regions drew 2.35 million visitors in 1999, an increase of 14 percent from the previous years. However, Morocco—like other tourist destinations—suffered a sharp decline in the number of visitors after the terrorist attacks of September 11, 2001, against the United States.

The state bank, the Banque al-Maghrib, plays a crucial role in the country's banking system. It has the authority to issue dirhams (the country's currency), maintain the foreign currency reserves (which cover up to six months of imports), control credit supply, oversee the government's specialized lending organizations, and regulate the commercial banking industry. The Casablanca Stock

The Economy of Morocco

Gross domestic product (GDP*): $33.73 billion (2001 est.)

GDP per capita: $1,180 (2001 est.)

Inflation: 1% (2001 est.)

Natural resources: phosphates, iron ore, manganese, lead, zinc, fish, salt

Agriculture (15% of GDP): wheat, barley, potatoes, sugarcane, olives, citrus, sugar beets, tomatoes, wine grapes, livestock (1999 est.)

Industry (33% of GDP): phosphate rock processing, food processing, leather goods, textiles, construction, cement (1999 est.)

Services (52% of GDP): transportation, communications, shipping, tourism (1999 est.)

Foreign trade:

Imports—$12.2 billion: industrial equipment, food, beverages and tobacco, semi-processed goods, consumer goods, fuel, chemical products (1999 est.)

Exports—$7.6 billion: phosphates and fertilizers, minerals, textiles, leather goods, citrus, canned fish, vegetables, seafood (2000 est.)

Currency exchange rate: 10.64 Moroccan dirhams = U.S. $1 (October 2002)

*GDP, or gross domestic product, is the total value of goods and services produced in a country annually.
Sources: CIA World Factbook, 2001; World Bank; U.S. Department of State FY 2001 Country Commercial Guide.

Exchange is the third largest in Africa after Johannesburg's and Cairo's.

ECONOMIC REFORMS AND CHALLENGES

Until 1992 the Moroccan government controlled most of the country's industry. Since then, there has been considerable movement toward privatization (the selling of state-owned enterprises to private-sector investors) and a broad range of economic reforms, including the devaluation of the currency and pricing regulations designed to encourage local production. Such changes to Morocco's economy have won the support of the World Bank and the International Monetary Fund. As of 2002, nearly 60 of the country's 114 state-owned enterprises had been sold, raising $1.7 billion. Plans were also on the table to privatize numerous hotels, banks, sugar plants, the state fertilizer company, part of the state telephone company, and a portion of Royal Air Maroc.

Morocco's Association Agreement with the European Union (EU), which began on March 1, 2000, calls for the gradual elimination of tariffs (taxes on imported goods) on Morocco-EU trade in

A selection of Moroccan notes and coins. The basic unit of currency in Morocco is the dirham; one dirham was worth just under 10 American cents as of October 2002.

industrial goods over the following 12 years, which should hasten Morocco's economic integration into Europe. The goal of the recent U.S.–North Africa Economic Partnership is to promote the Maghreb as a destination for U.S. business, and the United States as a market for Maghreb exports. Approximately 30 American franchises, such as Pizza Hut (the first franchise, established in 1992), McDonald's, Dunkin' Donuts, and Dairy Queen, have arrived in Morocco in recent years. Foreign investment has grown from $50 million to $2 billion in the past decade.

The Moroccan economy also has several other important, albeit less conventional, sources of income. These include money sent to family members from Moroccans working in other countries, as well as the illegal export of cannabis (marijuana and hashish), grown in the north.

The government faces the challenges of high unemployment—which in urban areas exceeds 22 percent—payments on a multibillion-dollar debt, and recurring drought. Criticism has been voiced over the slow pace of change, with the extensive government bureaucracy and the conflicting interests of numerous top ministers often being singled out as the culprits. Nonetheless, progress has been made. Mohammed VI has established a commission to improve foreign investment in Morocco, and efforts to liberalize the telecommunications market and other sectors are under way.

POLITICS AND GOVERNMENT

Morocco is a constitutional monarchy with a parliament and, at least officially, an independent judiciary. Under the nation's constitution, the king has ultimate authority. He is commander-in-chief of the Royal Armed Forces and has the power to appoint and dismiss the prime minister and the members of his cabinet. The king may dissolve the parliament at will. He promulgates laws, signs and ratifies treaties, and can pardon accused criminals. The Moroccan constitution also designates the king as the country's spiritual leader, *Amir al-Mu'minin* ("Commander of the Faithful"), thus conferring on him spiritual as well as temporal authority.

In September 1996 Morocco's constitution was amended by **referendum**, making the government somewhat more democratic, although the king still retains near-absolute power. A two-chamber parliament was organized. Its upper house, the 270-member Chamber of Advisors, is elected by trade unions, local councils, and professional associations; the 325-member lower house, the Chamber of Representatives, is directly elected by popular vote. Members of the Chamber of Advisors serve for nine years; members of the Chamber of Representatives serve for five. Parliament now may initiate and approve bills and legislation and establish committees to investigate government matters.

After legislative elections in 1997, a coalition government was formed the following year. Hassan II appointed as prime minister the longtime opposition leader Abderrahmane Youssoufi, whose Socialist Union of Popular Forces won the most seats in the elections. Youssoufi's ascent marked the first time in Moroccan history that an alliance of socialist, nationalist, and left-wing parties was

The current flag of Morocco dates back to the early days of the Alawite dynasty in the 17th century. The flag was a plain red banner until 1912, when the green five-pointed star (known as Suleyman's seal) was added. (Green is the traditional color of Islam.)

Members of Morocco's parliament gather for a session in Rabat. Although the bicameral assembly gives the people some voice in government, the king has near-absolute power—including the authority to dissolve parliament if he wishes.

designated to govern—albeit with the king's loyalists in key positions, and under the king's ultimate authority.

Many of Morocco's political parties were formed during the French protectorate to work for independence, such as the Istiqlal (Independence) Party and the Parti Democratique pour Independence (Democratic Party for Independence). The Mouvement Populaire (Popular Movement) was created soon after independence, and at least eight other parties have formed since the 1970s.

Local government is organized on three levels. At the top level, governors (appointed by the king) rule the 49 provinces and main urban prefectures. These include four provinces in the Western Sahara. The second level consists of rural districts and municipalities, ruled by *chefs de cercle* (literally, "heads of the circle"). The third level is that of rural communes and separate urban centers, governed by *qa'ids* and pashas. The Ministry of the Interior or the governors appoint the lower-level officials. At each level, a council elected by popular vote decides local issues. The minister of the interior, appointed by the king, has authority over all three levels.

The Supreme Court, the highest tribunal in Morocco, sits in the capital city of Rabat and supervises the courts of appeals, regional tribunals, magistrates' courts, and trial courts. The king appoints Supreme Court judges. Morocco has 15 courts of appeals. Local tribunals hear cases that involve small amounts of money. More important cases are tried in regional tribunals. There are also 14 labor tribunals.

As Morocco is an Islamic state, matters concerning the personal status of Muslims, such as domestic law and inheritance, are referred to **qadis**, Muslim judges who interpret Islamic law. Rabbinical law is applied to personal or religious Jewish questions.

In 1990 the minister for religious endowments proclaimed that Islamic law forbids a woman to exercise political power. The next year, women's groups presented a petition with a million signatures demanding changes to the *Moudawana*, or family code. Traditionally, only men could divorce—and they could do so at will. The petitioners asked that women also be given the right to divorce and that all divorces be handled solely through courts. They also wanted to abolish polygamy (multiple marriage) and to end rules requiring women to have male guardians (*walis*). Some revisions were enacted, but in 1996 women's groups restated their determination to reform fully the family code.

RELIGION

Islam is the cornerstone of Morocco's political, spiritual, and traditional social life. King Mohammed VI is a sharif, a descendant

Five times each day, a *muezzin* calls Muslims to prayer from the minaret of the Koutubia Mosque in Marrakech. Nearly all of the people of Morocco follow Islam.

The Hassan II Mosque in Casablanca is the largest Muslim religious monument in the world outside of Mecca. The mosque has space for 25,000 worshippers inside and another 80,000 outside. At 689 feet (210 meters) high, the mosque's minaret is the tallest in the world. It can be seen for miles—even at night, as the top photograph shows. The mosque, which took more than five years to build, was finished in 1993, in time for the 60th birthday of the former king of Morocco. Some 6,000 Moroccan artisans worked to create beautiful mosaics (such as the one at the bottom of the pool, left), as well as stone and marble floors and columns, sculpted plaster moldings, and carved wood ceilings.

of the prophet Muhammad. He is the ultimate spiritual authority in Morocco (the "Commander of the Faithful") and is empowered to interpret the laws of Islam. His combined religious and political roles make him the supreme arbiter of Moroccan public life. The country's constitution proclaims, "Islam is the religion of the State which guarantees to all the freedom of worship."

The population of Morocco is 98.7 percent Muslim; most belong to the Sunni sect, Islam's dominant branch. Only 1.1 percent of Morocco's people are Christians, and of that group most are Roman Catholic. Jews account for just 0.2 percent of the population.

Islam arrived in North Africa in the mid-seventh century, but did not reach Morocco until near the latter part of the century. The slow, drawn-out process of Islamicization in Morocco began to take root around 710 following the capture of Tangier. With the combination of conquests and trade, more and more Berbers became Islamicized.

Today, individual religious practice varies between the city and the country, the liberal and the traditional, the Berber and the Arab. However, there is a clear pride in, and devotion to, Islam throughout Morocco.

For years neighboring Algeria has struggled with an **Islamist** movement—which seeks to impose a strict, conservative interpretation of Islam on society and government. Much violence has resulted. Islamic fundamentalism is weaker in Morocco, though socioeconomic inequality could fuel the Islamist movement's efforts to create a more observant and rigorously Islamic society and state. Throughout most of King Hassan's reign, Islamists were outlawed and arrested. But toward the end of his reign controls were loosened and a moderate Islamist party was encouraged to participate in parliamentary political life. Perhaps as a result of this element of toleration, the leaders of Morocco's main Islamist groups—unlike their counterparts in Algeria—advocate nonviolence in building an

Islamic state.

The Christian population in Morocco consists mainly of ethnic French, Spanish, and Italians who established roots during different waves of migration and colonization. They reside, for the most part, in port cities. In 1956 Christians in Morocco numbered about a half million; today the Christian population is approximately 60,000.

Although tiny today, the Jewish community in Morocco has a long and illustrious history. There is no record of exactly when the first Jewish communities were established in Morocco, but their roots go back to ancient times. Inscribed stones from the third century A.D., found at the Roman site of Volubilis, are the oldest archaeological evidence of Morocco's Jewish past. Many Jews originally settled in Ifrane, in the Anti Atlas Mountains, where they lived until the 1960s.

It is thought that some Berbers who lived and worked with the Jews during Roman times converted to Judaism. In a cross-fertilization of beliefs, the Jews of Morocco began to venerate saints and demons, a Berber practice. Jews and Berbers fought the Muslim invasion side by side. There is a story (which may or may not have much basis in history) of a Jewish priestess named Kahina who led a tribe of Jewish Berbers in a battle against seventh-century Arab invaders.

Under Islamic law, the sultan was required to protect the Jewish people. But from the 11th century on, Jews, while officially considered *dhimmis* (protected people), were second-class citizens. Jews had to pay a special poll tax, could not ride horses or own weapons, and in some towns had to remove their shoes when passing a mosque. Jews had, and still have today, their own rabbinic courts to decide questions of contracts, finance, personal issues, and inheritance, as well as the freedom to practice Judaism. The French protectorate eliminated the second-class status of the Jewish population but left their legal and political position ambiguous.

Beginning with the formation of the State of Israel in 1948 and continuing into the 1960s, the majority of the country's 280,000 Jews resettled in Israel. Today, approximately 4,000 to 5,000 Jews remain in Morocco; most reside in Casablanca, with smaller communities in Fez, Rabat, and Marrakech. Their religious practice combines Berber, Oriental, Arab, and Spanish customs, which distinguishes them from eastern European Jews.

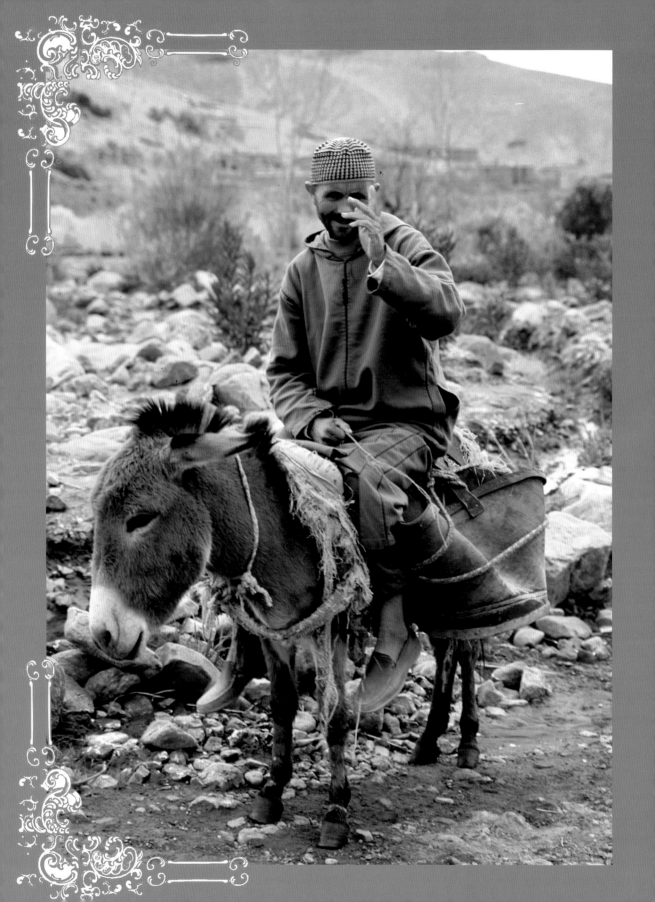

A Moroccan man, in traditional garb, rides a burro.

The People

Morocco's population in 2001 was estimated at 30,645,305—a bit smaller than that of the state of California. Nearly half of the people live in cities, and that proportion continues to increase. Overall, Morocco's population is growing slightly faster than that of countries outside of Africa, but the rate is below the average for Middle Eastern countries. More than one-third of the country's population is under 15 years of age.

LANGUAGE

The majority of Moroccans descend from the Berber communities, but generations of intermarriage with the Arab population and assimilation into the dominant Arab-Islamic culture have somewhat blurred the differences between Arabs and Berbers. In the early 19th century there were clear linguistic differences between the Berber-speaking tribes of

A walled Berber village in Morocco. Each of the small fortresses (*kasbahs*) in this village housed a family. Some parts of this village, which guarded an ancient trade route across the Sahara, are more than 900 years old.

the countryside and mountains and the urban Arabic elite. Today, an estimated 40 to 45 percent of the population speaks Berber. Of that group, between 75 and 90 percent also speak Arabic, to a greater or lesser degree. In recent decades, a steady exodus of Berber speakers from rural areas into urban centers, as well as the increasing extension of state authority and education to the mostly mountainous rural areas, intensified and diversified the nature of Berber-Arab interactions, with contradictory effects. On the one hand, Arabic has spread among the Berbers. On the other hand, there is a growing movement in Morocco—and in Algeria and among North African emigrant communities in Europe and North

America—to preserve and cultivate a self-conscious Berber identity. Organizations have been formed to study Berber culture, literature, and oral traditions. In Algeria, the Berber question has an overt political dimension as well.

The Berber language still exists in its original forms, particularly in the mountain regions. Berber speakers are divided into three ethno-linguistic groups: Berbers in the Rif Mountains, who speak Riffian (*Tarrifit*); the Tamazight speakers in the Middle Atlas (Tamazight is also the name used to denote the Berber language as a whole); and those who speak Tashelhit (*Shluh*) in the High Atlas and Sous Valley.

Arabic, the official national language, is spoken by most Moroccans, though French is a strong second language and is often used for business, government, diplomacy, and academic research publications. The educated upper class also studies and speaks English. In addition, Spanish is still spoken in the northern areas formerly under Spanish rule, and in the Spanish enclaves of Ceuta and Melilla.

GIRLS AND BOYS IN MOROCCAN SOCIETY

What is it like to grow up in Morocco? Anthropologist Susan Davis's study of a north-central town in the mid-1970s describes a patrilineal society (that is, a society in which descent is traced through the male line), where male babies are favored over females. Daughters marry, move from their home to their husband's family dwelling, and are "lost to the family"; grown sons are responsible for the support of their elderly parents.

Davis noted that the birth of a boy is celebrated with a more elaborate naming ceremony than that of a baby girl. Until age two, however, there is little difference in the treatment of males and females. But during early childhood, fathers are more attentive to their sons than their daughters. At about five years of age, girls

Berber children walk together. Girls and young women are permitted greater freedom today than they traditionally had in the past; however, in Morocco's Islamic society women are considered subservient to men.

contribute to the household chores: they wash dishes, attend to errands, sweep, and care for younger siblings. Boys may help with the occasional errand, but they do not participate in most domestic matters.

During this stage of development children are introduced to the concept of proper behavior or *hshim*, which is literally translated as "show some shame!" or "behave!" For boys this means learning to sit quietly; for girls it also requires physical modesty.

In later childhood, between the ages of 6 and 12, girls learn the basics of housework and child care. They are responsible for household errands but are not allowed to go out freely because of the importance of maintaining honor (which is equated with sexual purity). At this stage they learn *qul*, more mature behavior. Boys do not acquire this quality until much later; they pass their days outside the home with friends, unsupervised, playing soccer and attending public school. Boys are more boisterous and freer than girls during these years.

Between the ages of four and eight, Moroccan boys undergo *tahar*, or circumcision. Based on Davis's study, this often occurs with little or no warning or explanation, unless older male siblings or friends have alerted them. Circumcision is an important milestone; friends and relatives are invited to celebrate before, rather than after, the operation, in case the boy becomes ill and his mother needs to attend to him. The festivities center on the boy, the way a girl is the focus of attention at her wedding.

In adolescence boys enjoy much freedom, while girls have limited social lives. Boys are expected to develop *qul* in their early twenties, then move on to become responsible members of Moroccan society.

Many of the customs described in Davis's study still survive almost 30 years later, especially in rural areas. However, since her study, important changes have occurred. While girls' status is still not equal to that of boys, their value in the family has increased as they become more educated and engage in work outside the home. By the mid-1990s women made up 25 percent of the urban workforce, although their average wages were considerably lower than men's. Today, some Moroccan women serve as doctors, judges, engineers, scientists, bus drivers, and merchants. Several decades ago girls in Muslim countries married in early adolescence. Today, the average marrying age for young women in rural areas is 19, much later in urban areas. Moroccan men marry around the age of 28.

The progress of women in Moroccan society, however, has been slow. As a modern state, Morocco is a member of the United Nations and a signer of the Universal Declaration of Human Rights, which affirms equal rights for men and women in all aspects of marriage and divorce. The Moroccan constitution stipulates that "men and women shall enjoy equal political rights." But women's freedom continues to be limited, as Morocco is a Muslim state, under Islamic family law. The renowned Moroccan sociologist Fatima Mernissi explains: "What was, and is still, at issue in Morocco . . . is not an ideology of female inferiority, but rather a set of laws and customs that ensure that women's status remains one of subjugation. Prime among these are the family laws based on male authority."

EDUCATION

School is free and mandatory (required) in Morocco for six years, at the primary level from age 7 to 13. In 1999, 79 percent of children in this age group (83 percent boys; 74 percent girls) were enrolled in primary school. Secondary school enrollment dropped to 38 percent (43 percent boys; 33 percent girls). The number of children who attend school decreases dramatically outside the cities. Rural areas suffer a shortage of schools and teachers, and many boys stay home to help farm the land. Even less importance is placed on girls' education, and they too remain at home. In 1999 adult illiteracy in Morocco was among the highest in the Arab world, at approximately 48.3 percent (33.8 percent for men; 61.9 percent for women). In rural areas, illiteracy may reach 90 percent among girls. The Moroccan government has been making efforts to remedy this situation: education accounted for 21.3 percent of the country's entire 1999–2000 budget.

Approximately 230,000 students attend Morocco's state universities, including the nation's largest, Mohammed V University in

Opposite: This map illustrates the distribution of Morocco's population. The greatest concentrations of people occur around settlements along the coast, although there are areas of heavy population on the edge of the Sahara Desert, such as around Tagounit and Taouz.

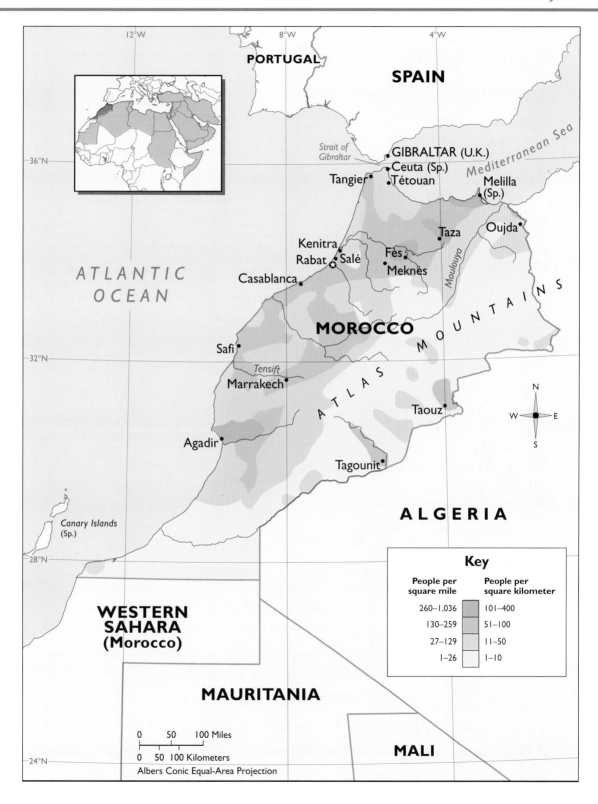

PORTUGAL

SPAIN

12°W

8°W

4°W

36°N

Strait of
Gibraltar

GIBRALTAR (U.K.)
Ceuta (Sp.)
Tangier
Tétouan

Melilla
(Sp.)

Mediterranean Sea

Taza

Oujda

Kenitra
Rabat
Salé

Fès
Meknès

Casablanca

ATLANTIC
OCEAN

Moulouya

MOROCCO

M O U N T A I N S

32°N

Safi

Tensift

Marrakech

A T L A S

Taouz

N

W   E

S

Agadir

Tagounit

ALGERIA

Canary Islands
(Sp.)

28°N

Key

People per
square mile

People per
square kilometer

260–1,036
130–259
27–129
1–26

101–400
51–100
11–50
1–10

WESTERN
SAHARA
(Morocco)

MAURITANIA

0   50   100 Miles

0   50 100 Kilometers

Albers Conic Equal-Area Projection

24°N

MALI

The People of Morocco

Population: 30,645,305

Ethnic groups: Arab-Berber, 99.1%;
　European, 0.7%; Jewish, 0.2%

Religions: Muslim, 98.7%; Christian,
　1.1%; Jewish, 0.2%

Age structure:
　0–14 years: 34.39%
　15–64 years: 60.93%
　65 years and over: 4.68%

Population growth rate: 1.71%

Birth rate: 24.16 births/1,000 population

Death rate: 5.94 deaths/1,000 population

Infant mortality rate: 48.11 deaths /
　1,000 live births

Life expectancy at birth:
　total population: 69.43 years
　males: 67.2 years
　females: 71.76 years

Total fertility rate: 3.05 children
　born/woman

Literacy: 43.7% (1995 est.)

All figures are 2001 estimates unless otherwise indicated.
Source: CIA World Factbook, 2001

Rabat, which has branches in Casablanca and Fez. The Hassan II Agriculture and Veterinary Institute, also located in Rabat, is acclaimed for its social science research as well as its science programs. Located in Ifrane, Al-Akhawayn is Morocco's only private university and has the distinction of being the first English-language university in North Africa. It enrolls approximately 1,000 students. The renowned Qayrawin University in Fez is one of the oldest centers for Islamic study. In addition to these schools, there are numerous technical schools and institutes of higher learning throughout the country.

HOUSING AND DAILY LIFE

In Casablanca and other Moroccan cities, wealthy residents live in large Mediterranean-style villas and modern apartment buildings. Members of the middle class usually reside in more modest attached or semi-attached homes. Many of the country's urban poor live in **bidonvilles**, shantytowns on the outskirts of the cities. *Bidons* are flattened tin cans that are used to build simple shacks. Bidonvilles developed during colonization when the medinas, the original urban centers, could no longer accommodate the increasing influx of people from rural areas.

In the country, houses may consist of a single room that serves as a kitchen, living room, bedroom, and barn. Depending on the climate and resources, these houses are often built of wood and stone, or dried mud bricks.

In the traditional Moroccan home, widowed parents often live with their married sons and families. Social life centers on the home and family; sidewalk cafés are filled with men in rural villages, and with men and women in the cities. Urban and rural Moroccans also participate in various religious celebrations and festivals throughout the year. In the largest city, Casablanca, people amuse themselves by going to movies or to Internet cafés, shopping, eating out, watching or playing sports, or going to the beaches located just outside of town.

European sports were introduced at the end of the 19th century; before then horsemanship and hunting were the traditional national pastimes. Football (what Americans call soccer) is now the favorite sport to watch and play. Polo, golf (Morocco's first golf course was built in Tangier in 1914), swimming, and tennis (the country fielded its first Davis Cup team in 1999) are also popular. In 1970 Morocco became the first African country to participate in soccer's World Cup. Morocco has also developed a tradition in track and field. At the 1984 Los Angeles Olympics two Moroccans won gold medals in track and field events. One of them was Nawal Al Moutaouakkil, winner of the 400-meter hurdles. She was the first Moroccan ever to win an Olympic medal, and the first woman from an Islamic country to take home the gold. Hicham al-Guerrouj, the world's premier middle-distance runner, holds many world records.

CLOTHING

In the 1930s, French artist Jean Besancenot traveled throughout Morocco studying the costumes of the men and women of the

Maghreb. He created 60 paintings and many drawings of Moroccan jewelry, clothing, ornaments, and tattoos, which were published in an impressive 1940 volume, *Costumes et Types du Maroc*. Besancenot noted the various cultural and historical influences on Moroccan dress, and he studied the details, materials, and significance of the many costumes. Each style of rural dress represented a tribal identity through fabrics, color, and draping—sometimes handed down since Roman times. In urban centers, clothing styles were derived from the Arabic styles introduced with Islam in the seventh century. The Jews of Morocco wore costumes whose styles were influenced by the clothing of Palestine and Spanish Andalusia, their earlier homelands.

Today traditional clothing is still worn throughout the country, though in cities and towns people also wear Western clothing or a combination of Western and traditional styles. The traditional articles of clothing still worn by men in the city and country include the *jellaba*, a short-sleeved hooded robe, usually in earth tones and sometimes striped; the *selham*, a full sleeveless cloak with silk pom-poms on the hood; and the *burnoose*, a heavier version of the *jellaba*, often with embroidery around the hood, worn by men in the country and by wealthy men in the cities, whose dress may also include a silk robe called a *ghandooura*. Many men wear a skullcap or brimless cap; the fez, a hat named for the city of Fez, is red with a flat top and tassel and is worn for formal events.

When in public, some city women still wear the *haik*, a large piece of woolen or cotton fabric that acts as a hood, cloak, and veil, to completely cover the body. Since independence in 1956, however, women, as well as men, also wear the *jellaba* as an outer garment. At home, a long, lightweight robe called a caftan is popular. In the countryside, Berber women weave their own cotton and wool to make the *izar*, a long, flowing piece of draped cloth, worn in a manner similar to ancient Greek and Roman garments; and the *hendira*, a blanket-like shawl. Some women in rural communities continue to wear the veil. And since a resurgence of religious activism beginning in the 1990s, many young, career-oriented women in the cities have chosen to cover their head with a scarf.

TRADITIONAL HANDICRAFTS

The arts and crafts of Morocco reflect age-old designs and the influences of many great civilizations. Throughout history the country has maintained the rich artistic heritage that grew from its Berber, Islamic, Middle Eastern, Jewish, Mediterranean, and European roots. Morocco, a fertile crossroads of culture, knowledge, design, and trade, continues to promote its artisanal tradition.

This woven textile contains the bright colors and geometric patterns common to traditional Berber weavers in Morocco.

A stroll through the medina of Fez reveals a vast selection of handicrafts. There is a leather market where skins are stored before dying. Stalls sell yellow embroidered leather slippers and belts layered with gold or silver, inspired by traditional Moorish and Levantine (eastern Mediterranean) art. Dark silk embroideries whose intricate work recalls the designs of Asia Minor and the Balkans are sold in other shops along the narrow, winding streets. In one part of the ancient market, carpenters create finely carved coffee tables, cupboards, and chests. In other quarters copper-smiths sell cauldrons and large trays used for celebrations, and dye merchants display colorful wools, cottons, and silks. In the Andalusian area, where a large chimney marks the pottery market, intricately designed ceramics, colored in traditional blues, browns, greens, and yellows, may be found.

In the port city of Essaouira woodworkers and cabinetmakers decorate *thuya* wood with inlays of lemon tree wood, mother-of-pearl, ivory, or silver. The town of Tiznit in the south, a stopping point for the desert nomads who inhabit the Anti Atlas and Souss regions, has a jewel market where goldsmiths create tiaras, pendants, and brooches inspired by old Moorish designs, as well as stalls where merchants sell colorful traditional clothing.

Rural and urban arts and crafts in Morocco differ in several ways. Urban art objects are decorated to celebrate and honor the

In Morocco, many artisans use traditional methods, rather than modern technology. The tannery in Fez, where animal skins are still treated using 900-year-old methods, is an example. Animal hides are taken to the Tanner's Quarter, as the picture at left shows. At the tannery (opposite), the skins are treated and dyed in round pools filled with chemicals, then spread out over nearby roofs (or any open area) to dry.

Islamic religion: verses from Islam's holy book, the **Qur'an** (also spelled "Koran"); the 39 names of Allah (the Supreme Being); and Islamic patterns and calligraphy grace the arts and crafts of different towns. These religious symbols, originally used to decorate mosques and palaces, were eventually applied to ceramics, textiles, jewelry, and woodwork. In keeping with Islamic law, humans or animals are seldom depicted. The Islamic designs are themselves an act of worship and meditation, the artisan's tribute to Allah.

A colorful and intricate tile pattern. Morocco is known for its ceramic tile designs. Because Islam does not allow living things such as people, animals, or plants to be depicted in art, artists often decorate buildings with detailed geometric patterns.

In the 17th and 18th centuries, urban artisans worked full-time for the sultans, decorating the mosques and palaces; today they work full-time for the elite and the tourist market. Artisans work in specific neighborhoods and belong to well-organized guilds. Held to exacting standards, a young apprentice must receive the formal approval of the *maalem*, or master artist, before he can work for himself. Although there are some regional variations, every craft has its own specific requirements and Arab-Muslim identity that must be maintained.

In rural areas of Morocco, where farming and herding prevail, art is utilitarian, yet often beautiful and creative. Rural craft techniques—unlike those fostered by the apprentice system of urban guilds—are passed down through families and tribes and are not practiced full-time. Islam plays a smaller role in rural art, and designs tend to focus on nature, including celestial and harvest cycles. The Muslim taboo against human and animal representation is also less pronounced.

In both urban and rural areas textile production—namely, weaving and embroidery—is considered Morocco's greatest artistic tradition. It is one of the oldest North African crafts, arriving around 1500 B.C. with the Berbers, whose weaving techniques were used for religious, magical, and practical purposes. Morocco's decorative textiles developed through the centuries into a world-renowned art form.

FOLKLORE, FOOD, AND FEASTS

Morocco has a deep and expressive tradition of folklore. In this land rife with tales of spirits, genies, magic, and mystery, there are age-old stories and superstitions that pertain to almost every situation. Cooking, feasts, hospitality, and celebrations are essentials of Moroccan life, rooted in the culture and character of the people. Throughout the ages, the importance of food has provided fertile ground for myth and superstition.

Dr. Francoise Legey, a French doctor, published a book in 1926 about Moroccan folklore. During her 15 years in Morocco, first with the Ministry of Foreign Affairs, then as a doctor, she was immersed in Moroccan life, from the nomadic tribes of the desert to the palace of the sovereign. In *The Folklore of Morocco* she describes the sacred, powerful role of food:

> Only one person is supposed to portion out the bread at table. If anybody else were to cut the loaf again, and to offer some more bread, it is thought to mean that a pretext for a quarrel is being sought for.
>
> Yeast is never sold after three o'clock in the afternoon, for it would mean giving away the luck of the house. If yeast is borrowed, it should always be returned, otherwise one would get an eruption around the mouth.
>
> If milk is boiling and it gets burnt, it is a sign that the genie wanted some, and a saucerful should be offered to them.

Dr. Legey also wrote of *kimia*, a magical power that can increase the food crucial for one's life and fortune. The force of *kimia* was said to multiply oil, bread, meat, or almost any kind of nutriment. However, a person fortunate enough to attract this spirit could easily lose it merely by mentioning its presence to others.

Whether *kimia* could make foods multiply or not, generosity and abundance are key aspects of Moroccan cooking and hospitality. Even in homes where expensive meat and other ingredients are financially prohibitive, meals and *diffas* (banquets) will be prepared with lots of vegetables and grains to express a warm welcome. At *diffas* it is important to serve a lavish overabundance of food, as an extravagant feast is a point of pride for the host.

When a family hosts a *diffa*, friends, neighbors, and female relatives help with the lengthy preparation of special foods. In most homes cooking is considered women's work, and usually recipes are passed down from mother to daughter, and from mother-in-law

A Moroccan baker kneels before trays of flat bread and other goods at a public oven.

to daughter-in-law; cookbooks or written recipes are seldom used.

In the Moroccan home dining is a communal affair. People sit around a table, in the dining room or, in more modest homes, the living room, and after washing their hands, partake of a common dish. Food is traditionally eaten with the first three fingers of the right hand, and bread is used both as food and utensil to scoop up the food and sauces.

Bread is an important part of every meal; in many homes it is freshly baked every morning. The loaves are usually made with whole wheat or barley flour, mixed with baking flour. Round and somewhat dense, they have a slight taste of the spicy anise seeds used in baking. Bread kneaded and placed in a *gsaa*, an unglazed red clay pan, is often carried on the heads of children wearing padded caps to the community oven. The bread, branded with a wooden stamp that identifies the family, is returned to the homes when ready.

Couscous is Morocco's national dish. It is also the name of the grains of semolina that are steamed over a simmering stew made of vegetables and meat or fish, in a *couscousiere*, a type of double boiler that has an upper pot with a perforated bottom that allows the steam of the stew to cook the grain. Other grains, such as corn, millet, and barley, can also be used and served underneath the many different types of stew recipes. Three other popular dishes are *mechoui*, a Berber dish that consists of an entire lamb rubbed with garlic and ground cumin, then roasted on a spit; *bisteeya*, a large pigeon or chicken pie make with eggs, onions, and lemon sauce and sweetened with toasted almonds, layered within a very thin, flaky pastry; and *djej emshmel*, which is a stew of chicken, lemon, and olives. In the desert and outlying regions, camel, gazelle, hedgehog, and desert fox are part of the nomadic diet, as is a bread made from locusts.

Mint tea is enjoyed in cafés and homes throughout Morocco. A bunch of fresh mint is put in a teapot to steep with hot, sweetened green tea. The drink is then served in small, often ornately painted, glasses.

MUSIC

Throughout Africa and the Middle East music is everywhere—it streams from cafés, shops, car radios, and street musicians. Music is part of the religious, ceremonial, and everyday lives of the rich and poor. And in Morocco, as writer Philip D. Schuyler observed, "Each region, each city, and each social group has its own particular style of music, often performed on instruments unique to that group, with song texts sung in a highly specialized dialect."

Morocco's musical styles include classical Arab-Andalusian,

A Moroccan musician performs with *crotals*. These closed iron bells are hollow and contain a pellet that, when shaken, creates the instrument's rhythmic sound.

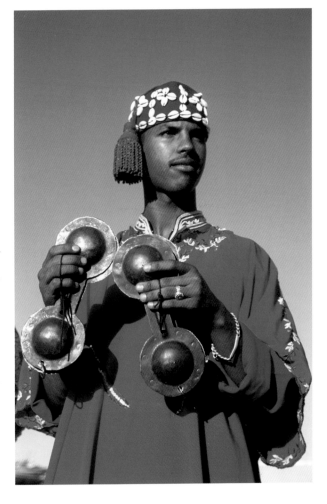

which developed in Muslim Spain in the ninth century, moved to Morocco at the end of the 15th century, and is now performed by orchestras in major cities; *Rai*, a popular, provocative form that started in Algeria in the 1960s and that mixes Arab-African rhythms, hip-hop, jazz, and rap; and Berber, a musical form of story-telling, often performed by wandering minstrels in small towns.

From the 1950s to the early 1970s, popular musicians from the United States (such as James Brown, Bob Dylan, and Jimi Hendrix), Egypt, France, and Lebanon led the commercial music scene. In late 1971 two new Moroccan groups, Nass el-Ghiwane and Jil Jilala, created a popular genre that merged traditional songs with folk and rock. In the process they became the most successful musicians in the country. Today, Moroccan musicians continue to explore their rich musical past and to fuse traditional Arabic and Berber music with the modern Western sounds of jazz, rock, and soul. *Rai*, rap, and rock music are all popular with Morocco's youth.

The view over Fez, an important spiritual and cultural center in Morocco. The city was founded in A.D. 789 by Idriss ben Abdallah, a descendant of Muhammad and the ruler who united the Arab and Berber cultures in the region and established Morocco's first ruling dynasty.

Communities

Morocco, a small country with a long history, is home to many cities and towns, each with its own ambiance, style, architecture, and crafts. With an estimated population of 3 million, Casablanca is the country's largest city. The cities of Rabat, Fez, Marrakech, and Meknès, founded as imperial capitals, continue to serve as political, spiritual, and historical centers. The Mediterranean and Atlantic coasts, the Rif and Atlas ranges, the center and eastern regions, and the southern desert lands all boast an intriguing array of Berber, Arab, nomadic, and mountain cultures.

TANGIER

A bustling, complex city that has been coveted and conquered by almost every power that has traversed the Mediterranean world, Tangier is the gateway to Morocco. Strategically located on the northwest corner of Africa, a few miles across the Strait of Gibraltar from Spain, this city of about 539,000 is closer to Europe than any other major city on the continent.

The first recorded history begins with the arrival of the Phoenicians, whose tombs still exist in the area. Under the Phoenicians, Tangier became a prominent trading port. After the fall of Carthage, Tangier became the capital of the independent kingdom of Mauritania. Subsequent conquerors included the Romans, Vandals, Byzantines, and Visigoths.

In A.D. 705 the Arab Muslims conquered Tangier with their newly converted troops of Berbers. They used the town as a base for their invasion of Spain. The Portuguese arrived next, and during the 15th and 16th centuries Tangier was ruled alternately by Portugal, Spain, and then Portugal again. The British received Tangier in 1662, along with Bombay in India, as a part of Catherine of Braganza's dowry as the new wife of King Charles II.

Morocco's Moulay Ismail seized Tangier in 1679; his ruthless harassment of the British colony led to the departure of the English in 1681. As a final good-bye, the British demolished most of the city.

An American consulate was established in Tangier in 1797. By 1856 Tangier was the diplomatic capital of Morocco, and by the late 19th century it had become an international mercantile and diplomatic center, visited by many European tourists. The French, Spanish, Italians, Germans, and British began to vie for control of the city—a problem partially solved by the 1906 Act of Algeciras, which conveyed the illusion of the sultan's sovereignty but in reality empowered the French. In the early 20th century, foreigners began to build villas on surrounding hills facing the sea. Their opulent lifestyle was in stark contrast to the poverty of the native Tanjawis who lived in the town below.

In 1923, under the Statute of Tangier, the city became an international zone, an unhampered, tax-free open port run by resident diplomatic agents from 10 countries, including Morocco. Each country managed its own banks, currency, and post offices and helped police the town. During this period exotic, freewheeling Tangier became a magnet for artists, writers, expatriates, adventurers, spies, and smugglers.

Soon after the country's independence from France, the Tangier international zone again became part of Morocco. Tangier's wild days subsided, as the city became a chic Mediterranean resort. In the 1950s and 1960s Tangier continued to be a destination for socialites, Beat poets, painters, and others charmed by its mystery and the allure of freedom.

Today, Tangier's economy is based on tourism. King Mohammed VI and his government, along with the European Union, have plans to develop the infrastructure of Tangier while curtailing the smuggling of illegal drugs and people, which has long plagued this North African port.

Tangier is a mix of Arabs, Berbers, and Europeans (mainly Spanish). Many residents are trilingual: fluent in Arabic, Spanish, and French.

RABAT AND SALÉ

Rabat, the royal city and capital of Morocco, is 172 miles (277 km) south of Tangier and 60 miles (97 km) north of Casablanca. Perched 100 feet (31 meters) above sea level, on a bluff overlooking the narrow Bou Regreg River, this thriving city was a small settlement and port of call for the Phoenicians and Carthaginians in the third century B.C. By the 10th century, near the ruins of the ancient Roman harbor, it became a *ribat*, a fortified community of Muslim warriors engaged in holy wars. The city prospered in the 12th century during the rule of the Almohad dynasty, which stretched from Tunisia to Moorish Spain. Although the Almohad dynasty collapsed centuries ago, many of the monuments of that period still stand, including the city's walls, its mosques, and the soaring—albeit unfinished—Hassan Tower, which rises to a height of 140 feet (43 meters).

Salé, Rabat's sister city on the opposite side of the river, became the most prosperous harbor in Morocco. In the 16th century, bold corsairs sailed from Salé to ravage distant shores and European vessels on the high seas in search of gold and slaves. During the 17th century residents of Rabat and Salé included Spanish and Muslim immigrants, Christian renegades, pirates, and adventurers. Rabat was again the capital, for a brief period, at the end of the 18th century. In 1912 Resident General Lyautey of France moved Morocco's capital city from Fez to Rabat, where it has remained.

Rabat is an orderly, modern urban center where Arabic and European, especially French, cultures coexist. Mediterranean-style villas, boutiques, embassies, and apartment buildings fill tree-lined boulevards near the historic medina. Men and women wearing contemporary fashions stroll the same streets as those in veils and traditional robes. Most Rabatis speak Arabic and French, and some speak Spanish as well.

The shallow waters of the Bou Regreg and the prosperous Casablanca harbor to the south have inhibited industrial growth in Rabat. However, the city is an important center of carpet and textile manufacturing, fish and fruit processing plants, and asbestos and brick production. Mohammed V University, the largest university in Morocco, is in Rabat.

In Salé, a traditional town just a few feet above sea level, craftsmen are known for their magnificent baskets. They also weave floor mats on large, horizontal looms using various reeds and grasses. In the medina, the city's noted *madrassa*, a beautifully restored 14th-century college, is a prime example of Moorish architecture. During the annual Festival of Candles, on the eve of Mouloud (the birthday of the prophet Muhammad), the people of Salé dress in embroidered period costumes and carry large, intricately decorated candles through the narrow streets to the shrine of Sidi Abdallah ibn Hassoun, patron saint of the city and of boatmen.

Rabat, including Salé, is the second-largest city in Morocco, with a population of about 1.5 million.

CASABLANCA

Morocco's largest city, Casablanca is a teeming, vibrant metropolis of about 3.2 million residents. Broad boulevards extend in star formation from the city center. Multistory apartment buildings, bustling business districts, and an active harbor define this cosmopolitan, almost European, city. As the industrial and commercial hub of the country, Casablanca hosts headquarters for more than half of Morocco's companies, and almost all of its major banks.

Originally a Berber state centered in the western suburb of Anfa, the region was conquered by Portugal in 1575. The Portuguese, who named Anfa "Casa Branca," remained until an earthquake destroyed the colony in 1755. The area never developed into more than a small village until the mid-1800s, when the Europeans returned and renamed the town Casablanca. The area began to grow and prosper, but the economic success of the Europeans caused resentment among the indigenous population. Violent uprisings led to the French invasion in 1907 and the eventual declaration of the French protectorate in 1912.

The French resident general Lyautey transformed Casablanca into the important economic center and symbol of Morocco that it is today. Despite fierce opposition, he developed the port, created new urban districts, expanded the railways, and laid out better roads. Architects designed graceful neo-Moorish and Art Deco buildings with white facades, columns, cedar wood balconies, wrought iron, and round cupolas. The city's rapid development and

Casablanca has been Morocco's major port since the French protectorate period; it is the country's largest city and an important center of economic activity.

promise of prosperity drew many people to Casablanca in search of work. However, unemployment became a problem and bidonvilles began to ring the city.

Today, the port of Casablanca is the city's economic center. Covering 445 acres (180 hectares), the port is protected from the Atlantic swell by the long Moulay Joussef Pier. It houses several docks, shipyards, a rail terminal, and a marina and dock for ferries and cruise ships. The port of Casablanca is one of the largest in Africa; it handles 70 percent of Morocco's shipping traffic and processes approximately 20 million tons of goods per year.

One of the city's striking new monuments is the Hassan II Mosque. Completed in 1993, it is among the largest religious buildings in the world. The Hassan II Mosque can accommodate more than 100,000 people—25,000 in the mosque, 80,000 on a huge esplanade. At 689 feet (210 meters), it boasts the world's tallest minaret, which is crowned with a laser that beams green rays, visible for 20 miles (32 km), toward Mecca. Constructed on a filled embankment that reaches into the Atlantic, the mosque affords worshippers a view of the ocean waves beneath its glass floor. The Hassan II Mosque is said to fulfill a verse in the Qur'an that reads, "the throne of god was built on water."

Casablanca is a major transportation hub. Modern highways connect it with other important cities in Morocco, a major railway system travels northeast to Algeria and Tunisia, and international airlines serve the city's Anfa and Novaceur airports.

Important industries include textiles, food canning, beer and soft drink production, leather working, and electronics. There is also commercial fishing from the city's coastal waters.

ESSAOUIRA

In the seventh century B.C. the small coastal town of Essaouira, southwest of Casablanca, was a regular stopping point for Phoenician shipping vessels. During Roman times, the town's scattered offshore islands—the Isles Purpuraires, or Purple Islands—were renowned for the purple dyes extracted from the shellfish murex, which was dug from their sands. Because purple was the imperial color, King Juba II had a dye factory built on one of the islands in the first century A.D. During the Middle Ages the port was a prominent link in the trans-Saharan caravan route. Ivory, gold, ebony, ostrich plumes, and gum arabic were unloaded, then shipped to England. At the close of the 15th century, Portugal seized the small port town, named it Mogador, and built a fort near the water. A few years later, the Sa'adians captured Mogador and Agadir, a coastal town to the south.

In the mid-1700s the Alawite sultan Mohammed ben Abdallah hired a French engineer to redesign Mogador to rival the port of Agadir. The new town, renamed Essaouira (meaning "little ramparts"), laid out on a grid system and surrounded by ramparts, became an important shipping link between Timbuktu (in present-day Mali) and Europe. The sultan ordered the European consuls in Agadir and Salé, along with the richest people in the kingdom, to relocate to Essaouira. Essaouira became the only city in the country where the Jewish population outnumbered the Muslims.

In 1912 the French renamed the city Mogador again, and during the colonial period its commercial role declined. After the French protectorate the town—again called Essaouira—became known for its relaxed ambiance, whitewashed houses with blue doors, colorful fishing boats, sandy beaches, and, more recently, superb windsurfing. The Purple Islands are now a falcon sanctuary. Orson Welles shot several scenes of his award-winning film *Othello*

Two views of Essaouira appear on these pages: (left) a colorful souk; (opposite) the medieval Portuguese fort that overlooks the harbor. Essaouira is a coastal town with a history that dates back more than 2,600 years. It has also been called Mogador at various points in its history.

here, and Jimi Hendrix, as well as other musicians and artists, frequented the city.

Today Essaouira, with a population of more than 440,000, is the home of hundreds of craftsmen who use *thuya* wood to create chess sets, furniture, jewelry, boxes, and bowls that are sold in souks or shipped overseas. *Thuya* trees, which grow on the sandy Atlantic coastline just outside the town, look like scrub oaks and sport wood that varies in color from dark mahogany to light buff.

The town's annual *Gnaoua* ceremony is a ritual procession practiced by descendants of Guinean slaves brought to Morocco from Central and West Africa. This folkloric event is said to have originated when one of the Guineans cured Fatima, the Prophet's daughter, by playing the *crotals* (iron castanets). Healer-musicians celebrate this event with a lively parade through the city, ending with a *mlouk*, when supernatural spirits are invited to join in a trance. The ceremony, part of a weeklong music festival, takes place in Essaouira every June.

AGADIR

Modern, sun-filled Agadir, with a population of more than half a million, is considered the premier seaside resort in Morocco and one of the country's most popular tourist destinations. After a devastating earthquake in 1960, Agadir was rebuilt for the tourist trade; it serves as a starting point for excursions into the towns and desert to the south. The town also boasts one of Morocco's leading fishing ports.

The port of Agadir was established in 1503 by a Portuguese nobleman. It was soon sold to the Portuguese government, which developed it into a busy commercial port and hub for caravans. Agadir became the capital of the Souss region, land of the **marabouts** (holy men) and homeland of the Sa'adians, who expelled the Portuguese in 1542. In 1769 Sultan Mohammed ben Abdallah, upset that Agadir had evolved into a rowdy center for military men, sailors, and merchants from across Europe, closed the harbor to European trade and created a rival port in Essaouira.

FEZ

The oldest of the imperial cities, Fez remains the spiritual center of Morocco. Originally it was a Berber town. Idriss I founded the present city—now the fourth largest in Morocco, with a population of about a million—in A.D. 789. In 809 his son, Sultan Idriss II, declared Fez the capital of the dynasty. An estimated 8,000 Muslims arrived in 818, fleeing the Christian armies of Andalusia, Spain. They settled on the east bank of the Oued Fez, where they contributed their worldly sophistication and intellectual vigor to the city life. Seven years later, the population grew as Arabs and Jews from Kairouan, Tunisia—mostly educated, successful craftsmen and merchants—located on the opposite bank. In 859 a Tunisian woman, Fatma ben Fihria, founded Kairaouine University, and her sister, Maria, founded the Kairaouine Mosque, which remain standing today.

Fez was plagued by chaos and famine until it was conquered in 1069 by the Almoravid sultan Youssef ben Tachfin. Later it was captured by the Almohads, who ruled in the mid-12th century.

When the Marinids conquered Fez, the city again became the capital of Morocco. During their reign, Fez reached its architectural and intellectual apogee as ornate palaces and elaborate *madrassas* graced the city. A new city, called Fez el-Jdid, was built in 1276 outside the walls of Fez al-Bali, the old town, as a military settlement and administrative base. To this day, the part of Fez outside the walls is called the "new" city, even though it is more than 700 years old.

This ornate golden door, set into a *zellij* (tile) wall, can be found at the royal palace in Fez, one of four imperial cities in Morocco.

Throughout the 19th century Fez remained the intellectual and spiritual heart of the country. The treaty declaring Morocco a protectorate of France, signed in Fez on March 30, 1912, led to riots in the city's streets. The city became a center of anti-colonialist sentiment and the birthplace of Morocco's Istiqlal (Independence) Party.

Fez el-Bali, among the world's largest thriving medieval cities, has the largest medina in Morocco. A seemingly endless maze of winding streets is lined with mosques, markets, workshops, and merchants selling crafts and food. The United Nations Educational, Scientific, and Cultural Organization (UNESCO) classified Fez's medina a world heritage site in 1976 and established a restoration program to reverse extensive damage due to age and overpopulation.

Since the early 1990s, this ancient spiritual stronghold has hosted the annual Fez Festival of World Sacred Music. For nine days in the spring, musicians from around the world perform sacred music from a wide array of religious traditions. From Sufi whirling dervishes, Berber trance music, and Javanese gamelan to 15th-century Italian folk music, 18th-century South African Zulu chorales, and 20th-century American gospel, the festival continues to enlighten and entertain.

A short distance southeast of Fez is the Berber town of Sefrou, home of the annual Cherry Festival. Every June this colorful folkloric event celebrates the return of the cherries with a procession to the tomb of the prophet Daniel, followed by folk dances and songs.

MEKNÈS

The imperial city of Meknès (population: 633,000), famous for the best olives in Morocco, is perched on a plateau, surrounded by lush plains of wheat, beans, cereals, grapes, olives, and citrus. In the 10th century the Zenata Berbers from the Meknassa tribe settled in this fertile region. When Moulay Ismail became sultan in 1672, he made Meknès his capital. Ismail surrounded the city with 16 miles (25 km) of thick walls and began an extensive building program that included his lavish palace. He ruled for 55 years. After his death in 1727, the imperial city was left unfinished and the glory of Meknès faded.

The French made Meknès into their military headquarters in 1912. Today, the agriculturally rich city is a railroad hub and producer of textiles, canned foods, cement, and vegetable oils. Meknès is still surrounded by walls 12 feet (4 meters) thick. The main entrance, the Bab el-Mansour, is considered the most exquisite gate in North Africa. The mausoleum of Moulay Ismail, resting place of the 17th-century sultan, is one of the few Moroccan shrines that may be entered by non-Muslims.

MARRAKECH

Located on the fringes of the desert in the western foothills of the High Atlas Mountains, the imperial city of Marrakech is Morocco's third-largest city, with a population of approximately 1.5 million. Twice it has served as Morocco's capital. This walled

This gate in the walls around Meknès shows traditional Moorish architecture. Today Meknès has the largest Berber population in Morocco.

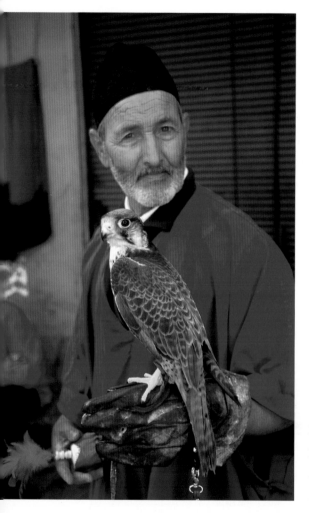

A man holds a falcon in Marrakech. For those who can afford it, falconry is a popular sport in Morocco, as it is in other Arab countries.

oasis city is a colorful, bustling, exotic threshold to the Sahara.

Marrakech was founded in 1062 by the Almoravid sultan Youssef bin Tachfin. The sultan's extensive development of Marrakech was continued after his death by his son, Ali, who constructed an elaborate underground irrigation system and a rampart of red earth and stone around the city. The protective wall measured 30 feet (9 meters) in height and extended for 5 miles (8 km). The Almohads overthrew the Almoravids and destroyed, then rebuilt, much of the city, including the famous Koutoubia Mosque. Considered one of the most noble and gracefully proportioned mosques in the western Muslim world, Koutoubia features a minaret that soars 220 feet (67 meters) into the air. In the 12th and 13th centuries, Marrakech was an important stop for caravans carrying gold, slaves, and ivory from Timbuktu to the Barbary Coast. Marrakech was the capital of Morocco until 1269, when the conquering Marinid dynasty ruled from Fez. The city again became the capital under the Sa'adians.

At the beginning of the French protectorate, Governor General Lyautey built a *ville nouvelle* (new city) outside of the old, and worked to restore the city's ancient medina and monuments.

Today, Marrakech is a glamorous ochre-colored city, renowned for its masterpieces of Moorish architecture and the lively Djemma el Fna Square, where jugglers, snake charmers, fortune-tellers, and dancers entertain the public.

The stalls in the busy, labyrinthine streets of the medina sell everything from carpets and slippers to pottery, perfumes, and spices. One of the most popular tourist destinations in Morocco, Marrakech is considered the capital of the south, although it is no longer a commercial, intellectual, or political center.

CELEBRATIONS, HOLIDAYS, AND FESTIVALS

Moroccans observe various secular, civic occasions as public holidays. Among the most important are New Year's Day, Throne Day (July 13), the anniversary of the Green March (November 6), and Independence Day (November 18). Yet in a country in which more than 98 percent of the people are Muslim, important Islamic holidays are almost universally celebrated and, frequently, serve as official public holidays as well.

Moroccan businesses and the government follow the Gregorian, or Western, calendar. But Muslim religious observances are based on the Islamic calendar, which begins in A.D. 622, the year Muhammad and his followers were forced to flee the Prophet's native city of Mecca, settling in Medina. (That event, considered the start of the Muslim era, is known as the Hegira or Hijra.) In addition, the Islamic calendar follows lunar cycles—specifically, each month begins when the crescent moon first becomes visible to a human observer after a new moon. Because the Islamic year is slightly longer than 354 days, Muslim holidays shift back with respect to the Gregorian calendar about 11 days each year. For example, the Islamic New Year fell on March 15 in 2002 (the year 1423 in the Islamic calendar), but in 2007 (1428 in the Islamic calendar) it will fall around January 21.

A Moroccan dancer performs at a public event in Rabat.

There are many Islamic holidays, but in Morocco, Eid al-Fitr and Eid al-Adha (the Feast of the Sacrifice) are most widely celebrated. As with Christmas in America, most of Morocco shuts down during each holiday so families and friends may be together to pray and join in the festivities. Eid al-Fitr marks the end of the holy month of Ramadan, which is observed by many Muslims with daylong fasts and evening feasts. Eid al-Fitr can last four to five days, during which people pray and enjoy festive meals. Eid al-Adha commemorates the patriarch Abraham's (Ibrahim's) sacrifice of the ram in lieu of his son Isma'il, according to Muslim tradition, and is observed in some towns with the ritual slaughter of a sheep.

Spiritual festivals called **moussems** occur around the same time as religious holidays such as Mouloud (the birthday of

Muhammad), Ramadan, and weddings. Celebrated throughout the country, *moussems* extol popular culture, promote commerce, and honor local saints. Music, dancing, feasting, traditional costumes, and markets where merchants sell crafts, produce, and camels highlight the celebrations. Some *moussems* include fantasias, spectacular war exercises and acrobatic feats conducted by men on horseback armed with antique rifles, which are fired in unison during a rapid gallop.

Every September, in the village of Imilchil in the Atlas Mountains, the Berber marriage *moussem* is held to introduce the semi-nomadic herdsmen to the village women. Almost 30,000 people of the Ait Hadiddou tribe and their subclans meet for the three-day celebration. On the first day, amid tambourine music and acrobatic performers, a trade fair takes place and the tomb of the holy man Sidi Mohammed el Merheni is honored. On the following days, the prospective brides and grooms, dressed in ornate, traditional clothing, briefly meet as the men walk in pairs through groups of women. If a man briefly acknowledges a woman and she replies with a nod, they seek family approval, then are married in a wedding tent by a representative of the Ministry of Justice.

From early spring to fall, festivals are held to celebrate the harvest. These lively, colorful events, which occur throughout the country, include the Almond Blossom Festival, Rose Festival, and Cotton Harvest.

On November 6, 1975, during the Green March, 350,000 unarmed Moroccans crossed the Moroccan border into the Spanish Sahara to claim sovereignty over the disputed territory. The status of the land now called Western Sahara remains the focus of a large part of Morocco's foreign policy.

Foreign Relations

Morocco, an Arab and Muslim nation in North Africa, maintains foreign policy interests in several regions, including the Mediterranean, Africa, and the Middle East. In addition, Morocco, a member of the United Nations and the World Bank, has traditionally enjoyed close relations with Europe and the United States.

Active in African, Arab, and Maghreb issues, Morocco is a member of the Arab League, the Arab Maghreb Union, and the Organization of the Islamic Conference. With Mauritania, Israel, Jordan, Tunisia, and Egypt, Morocco participates in the NATO Mediterranean Initiative, started in 1995. African affairs have proved stickier for Morocco: since 1984 Morocco has boycotted the Organization of African Unity (OAU) and its successor, the African Union (AU). The issue that precipitated the rift was the OAU's admission of the Saharan Arab

Democratic Republic (SADR), which contests Morocco's claim to the Western Sahara.

MOROCCO AND THE UNITED STATES

Morocco and the United States have enjoyed a friendly relationship since 1777, when Morocco became one of the first states to recognize American independence. Sultan Sidi Mohammed ben Abdallah, a progressive leader who ruled from 1757 to 1790, was aware of the economic benefits of good relations with Western countries. His plan was to develop the state-controlled maritime trade to generate revenue, and thus lessen his dependency on Morocco's professional army, which collected taxes and administered his authority. On December 20, 1777, the sultan issued a declaration stating that American vessels could freely enter Moroccan ports. He hoped that this would lead to a formal treaty of friendship with the United States.

The United States did not officially respond to the sultan until December 1780. At that time, however, America remained at war with Great Britain, while Morocco faced domestic problems of drought, famine, and inflation and diplomatic issues with Britain and Spain over the status of Gibraltar. As a result, further treaty negotiations were delayed for years. Finally, on October 11, 1784, the sultan's forces captured an American merchant ship and crew. Hoping to spur the delayed negotiations, Sidi Mohammed announced that the hostages and ship would be released only after a treaty with the United States was finalized. Serious negotiation began, and the Treaty of Friendship and Amity, also called the Treaty of Marrakech, was finally signed by the sultan on June 23, 1786, by Thomas Jefferson in Paris on January 1, 1787, and by John Adams in London on January 25, 1787. Ratified by Congress on July 18 of that year, the treaty, binding for 50 years, marked the start of diplomatic relations between the United States and Morocco.

Morocco's foreign minister, Mohamed Benaissa, shakes hands with President George W. Bush in the White House. The two leaders met in November 2001.

It was the first treaty between any Muslim, Arab, or African state and the United States. Renegotiated in 1836, it is still in effect and marks the longest unbroken treaty relationship in U.S. history.

An American consulate was established in Tangier in 1797. In 1821, in honor of the valued relationship between the two countries, Sultan Moulay Slimane, Sidi Mohammed's successor, gave the United States one of Tangier's most beautiful buildings for its diplomatic headquarters. Officially used from 1821 to 1956, and now a museum, it is the oldest diplomatic building owned by the United States in the world, and the only foreign property listed in the U.S. National Register of Historic Places.

Morocco became a French protectorate on March 30, 1912, and over the ensuing decades the U.S.-Moroccan relationship languished. In 1942, during World War II, the United States sent troops to Morocco and Algeria to combat the invasion of North Africa by the Axis countries of Germany and Italy. The following year, with North Africa secured, the Allies held a major conference in Anfa, on the outskirts of Casablanca. The 10-day Casablanca Conference—attended by Prime Minister Winston Churchill of Great Britain and President Franklin D. Roosevelt of the United

During the Second World War, Casablanca was the site of an important meeting of Allied leaders: (from left) French general Henri Giraud, U.S. president Franklin D. Roosevelt, French resistance leader Charles de Gaulle, and British prime minister Winston Churchill. At the Casablanca Conference, which was held secretly from January 14–24, 1943, the Allied strategy for winning World War II was set, with unconditional surrender by the Axis powers formally established as the Allied goal.

States, along with the leader of the Free French forces, Charles de Gaulle—produced a fateful strategic decision: that the Allies would insist on unconditional surrender from all their Axis enemies. During the conference, President Roosevelt—who enunciated the demand for unconditional surrender—also did something that would have ramifications for Morocco's postwar future. Roosevelt hosted a dinner in honor of Sultan Mohammed V and his son (later King Hassan II). Such recognition helped validate Morocco's goal of independence from France. Morocco gained independence on March 2, 1956.

During the Cold War, Morocco generally supported the United States and the Western European nations, while most other Arab countries were either neutral or sided with the Soviets. King Mohammed V proclaimed that the Treaty of 1836 would be upheld and confirmed his stand against communism. The United States elevated the status of its representative in Morocco from diplomatic agent to ambassador. In 1957 Mohammed V met with President Dwight D. Eisenhower in Washington, and, soon after, Vice President Richard M. Nixon visited the king to discuss bilateral cooperation. Mohammed V's son and successor, Hassan II, traveled to the United States at various times to meet Presidents Kennedy, Johnson, Carter, Reagan, Bush, and Clinton. King Hassan II's son, King Mohammed VI, met with President Clinton at the funeral of his father and made his first official visit to the United States in 2000.

The United States has encouraged Morocco to democratize, streamline its government, and improve its record on human rights. U.S. financial assistance for domestic, social, and economic programs from 1999 to 2001 was $88.1 million. The U.S. Agency for International Development (USAID) has been active in Morocco since 1953; the Peace Corps arrived in Morocco a decade later and now has more than 130 volunteers working in healthcare, education, agriculture, and environmental programs.

Morocco and the United States conduct joint military exercises. Morocco has granted the U.S. armed forces rights of transit through its airfields (which may also serve as an alternative landing site for the space shuttle). It also allows the U.S. Navy port visitation rights.

MOROCCO AND ISRAEL

Morocco's relationships with Israel and the Western nations have been complex since independence in 1956. For example, Morocco and the United States both opposed the French and British invasion of Egypt in 1956 after Egypt nationalized the Suez Canal. On the other hand, Morocco and the United States often disagreed about Israel. Generally, American policy strongly supports Israel, whereas Morocco—although expressing its views with moderation—has frequently sided with Israel's Arab neighbors and the Palestinians.

Morocco's historically large Jewish population added another element to the picture. King Mohammed V enjoyed a good relationship with the Jewish community, both within his own country and internationally. But beginning in the 1950s, many Moroccan Jews sought to emigrate, a large proportion of them wishing to settle in Israel. For economic and political reasons the Moroccan government initially opposed this. Four months after Moroccan independence, the Israeli migration office in Morocco was closed. On the other hand, Morocco wanted to become a member of the United Nations and needed American aid. Thus it needed to avoid the appearance of repressing its Jewish minority. Mohammed V's first cabinet was split over the issue of what to do about Jewish emigration. Finally the king decided to let those already in transit camps leave the country.

In 1958 Morocco joined the Arab League, which had been established in 1945 by seven Arab states: Egypt, Iraq, Lebanon, Saudi

In February 2001, foreign ministers from Morocco, Jordan, Syria, Egypt, Saudi Arabia, Tunisia, and Bahrain met with members of the Palestinian Authority. Like other Arab countries, Morocco has supported efforts to establish an autonomous Palestinian state, but its government has worked to facilitate a peaceful resolution to the violent Israeli-Palestinian conflict.

Arabia, Syria, Jordan, and Yemen. Again it became difficult for Jews to leave Morocco. Israel began secret efforts to smuggle Jews out through the Spanish enclaves and Gibraltar. One such operation met with disaster in January 1961, when a boat from Al Hoceima Bay, on the Mediterranean coast, capsized and 42 migrants drowned. Israel's efforts, however, were largely successful, and between 1957 and 1961 about 18,000 Jews left Morocco. By 1960 the country's Jewish community had decreased to approximately 162,000 from more than 211,000 in 1947. While approximately 30,000 Moroccan Jews resettled in the United States, Canada, and France, the majority immigrated to Israel. In the years to come, several Moroccan Jewish immigrants in Israel would become influential in their adopted country's diplomatic affairs with Morocco, helping to strengthen a frayed relationship.

In the 1970s King Hassan II was one of the first Arab leaders to encourage a political dialogue with Israel. Yitzhak Rabin, the Israeli prime minister, visited Morocco in 1976. This visit helped break ground for the Camp David Accords between Israel and Egypt in 1978. However, in 1979 Hassan, who had encouraged the Israelis and Palestinians to reach a compromise solution, became chairman of the new Jerusalem Committee, started by the Organization of the Islamic Conference. In this position, and as host of the 1982 Arab League summit in Fez, he helped advance a plan to dismantle the Israeli presence on the West Bank and create a Palestinian state. Morocco thus began to support a Palestinian homeland, bringing its policy closer to the positions of other Arab governments. Though Hassan's plan implied recognition of the existence of Israel, the Israeli government would not accept it. Throughout this period, however, Hassan maintained good diplomatic relations with the leadership of the moderate Israeli Labour Party. In 1986, when the Labour Party was in power, he invited Prime Minister Shimon Peres to his country for talks. The dramatic, public move would, Hassan hoped, advance the Arab-Israeli peace process.

In 1994, following diplomatic breakthroughs between Israel and the Palestinians, and Israel and Jordan, a Moroccan liaison office opened in Tel Aviv, and a reciprocal Israeli office opened in Rabat. The offices operated until fall 2000, when they were closed after the outbreak of sustained Israeli and Palestinian violence. U.S. secretary of state Colin Powell's first stop on his April 2002 trip to the Middle East to repair the deteriorating Israeli and Palestinian situation was Morocco. The day before his arrival, a pro-Palestinian demonstration in Rabat drew an estimated 500,000 to two million Moroccans. Nonetheless, the Kingdom of Morocco continues to support peaceful negotiations and moderation on both sides of the Israeli-Palestinian conflict.

MOROCCO AND THE WESTERN SAHARA

The unresolved conflict in the Western Sahara, a subject of internal and foreign concern, remains a crucial issue in Morocco's foreign affairs. After independence, Morocco was bordered by the Spanish-ruled Sahara and the French colonies of Mauritania and

Algeria. According to Moroccan nationalist doctrine, the historic Moroccan homeland includes parts of Algeria, Mauritania, and the Spanish Sahara. The Organization of African Unity took the position that the African countries should accept existing boundaries drawn up, however arbitrarily, by colonial powers. The United States and the OAU officially recognized Mauritania, an extremely poor, undeveloped land. Ten years later, in 1970, Morocco followed suit. Border demarcation with Algeria remained a contentious issue. But most problematic of all was the fate of the Spanish Sahara.

Now called the Western Sahara, this sparsely populated desert territory (74,000 adults in 1974, according to the Spanish census) borders the Atlantic Ocean between Mauritania and Morocco. It is rich in phosphates and has productive offshore fishing grounds.

After the Spanish departed in 1976, the area was divided between Morocco and Mauritania, but the latter gave up its territorial claims in 1979. This did not leave Morocco in full control of the Western Sahara, however.

In the early 1970s, even before the departure of Spain, a movement for Saharan independence had begun. Called the Polisario (Frente Popular para la Liberación de Saguia el Hamra y Rio de Oro), the group, backed by Algeria and Libya, demanded independence for the desert territory. UN representatives who arrived to ascertain the local population's preference were greeted by protesters waving Polisario flags and demanding the expulsion of Spain. Spain announced that it would transfer control of the area, but did not indicate to whom.

The issue went to the International Court, where lawyers for Morocco argued that there was a historical link between the Saharan tribes and the Moroccan sultans as their spiritual leaders. Mauritania also claimed a similar connection. The court agreed that despite historic links with the Spanish Sahara, neither Morocco nor Mauritania could claim sovereignty. It was decided that the people of the Spanish Sahara would be granted the right of self-determination.

On October 16, 1975, King Hassan II appeared on national television and asked the Moroccan people to volunteer to march peacefully across the border and claim the neighboring territory. On November 6 of that year, 350,000 unarmed Moroccans participated in what came to be called the Green March. They had the support of many Arab countries, the Palestine Liberation Organization, and Morocco's opposition parties. The United States did not object to the march, in part because American officials were concerned by the support Polisario was receiving from Algeria, a radical nation with anti-American leanings. As the Moroccans crossed the border, the Spanish army simply departed rather than fire on the thousands of unarmed Moroccan marchers. At this point, Spain was basically leaderless—its dictator, Francisco Franco, had collapsed on October 18 and would die on November 20. Spain had neither the desire nor the ability to maintain this remote colony.

On November 14 Spain, Morocco, and Mauritania announced a temporary agreement, under which the three countries would share administrative duties throughout the region, without deciding the question of sovereignty. Spain's role ceased the following year. In 1979, after Mauritania gave up its claim to the one-third of the territory it was holding following repeated armed attacks by Polisario, Morocco quickly extended its authority throughout most of the former Mauritanian-administered zone in order to preempt a Polisario takeover.

With Libyan and Algerian aid, Polisario had developed into a strong guerrilla force, and it won occasional battles against Morocco's well-equipped troops. But Morocco fought back, assisted by funding from Saudi Arabia, France, and the United States. Morocco eventually built a well-fortified earthen wall around 80

Polisario members wave their flags during an October 1975 demonstration for independence. Control of the Western Sahara territory has been disputed for decades.

percent of the territory where most of the Sahrawi people lived, to cement its control and neutralize Polisario's ability to mount raids.

The conflict affected Morocco's political relationships with other countries. By 1984 more than 70 nations had recognized the Saharan Arab Democratic Republic, the civilian wing of the Polisario, even though it existed only on paper, and it became a full member of the OAU. After withdrawing from the OAU in protest, King Hassan II reached out for support in the Arab world. Libya's leader, Colonel Muammar al-Qaddafi, agreed to cut off aid to the Polisario, and on August 14, 1984, Hassan II and Qaddafi signed a short-lived treaty of unity. Now the Polisario's only financial support came from Algeria. But even this support soon decreased, since Algeria was beset with its own economic problems. In 1988

Morocco and the Polisario agreed that the United Nations would supervise the reduction of troops in the region and organize a referendum. On September 6, 1991, a cease-fire began and a UN peacekeeping force was established.

The referendum, originally scheduled for January 1992, was designed to permit Sahrawis to determine whether they wanted to be part of Morocco or an independent state. However, it has been repeatedly postponed because of questions of voter eligibility; the referendum scheduled for 2002, a decade after the original date, was again delayed. Although the status of the Western Sahara remained unresolved as of 2002, Morocco claims sovereignty and administers most of the territory. King Mohammed VI upholds his father's position on this issue. The United States recognizes Morocco's administrative role but does not officially support the country's claim of sovereignty.

HUMAN RIGHTS AND THE WESTERN SAHARA

Amnesty International, a human-rights organization, reported in 1993 that, over the previous 15 years, more than 1,000 Sahrawis had disappeared after arrest by the Moroccan authorities. Unfortunately, disappearances of this type were common throughout Morocco (not just in the Western Sahara) from the early 1960s to the mid-1980s. Usually those who disappeared were locked up under harsh conditions in secret prisons, military jails, urban villas, and remote detention centers. After being arrested—or even after a trial and acquittal—Sahrawis who supported the Polisario or self-determination could vanish for weeks, years, or possibly forever, without a word to family or friends. After years of denying any knowledge of the disappearances, the Moroccan government released more than 270 prisoners in June 1991. Many of the released were Sahrawis who had been imprisoned for up to 19 years without a trial or contact with the outside world.

Since the mid-1990s, the Moroccan regime, under both Hassan and Mohammed, has made an effort to improve human rights in Morocco and the Western Sahara. A 1999 human-rights report issued by the U.S. Department of State maintained that for three consecutive years there were no new political disappearances in Morocco; in July 2000, the Moroccan government paid preliminary compensation to some victims.

MOROCCO AND ARAB AFFAIRS

Morocco is active in the African, Maghreb, and Arab spheres. Saudi Arabia and the Persian Gulf states provide Morocco with significant amounts of financial aid. In turn, King Hassan II sent approximately 1,200 Moroccan troops to defend Saudi Arabia against Iraq following the latter's 1990 invasion of Kuwait. Morocco was also the first Arab state to speak out against the Iraqi aggression.

Morocco's relationship with Algeria continues to be strained even though Algeria's involvement in the Western Sahara has lessened. This is partly because of other unsettled border issues and partly because of the Islamist movement in Algeria. Morocco's Islamist movement distances itself from the violent tactics of Algerian groups. In 1999, however, Algerian president Abdelaziz Bouteflika accused Morocco of providing a safe haven for Algeria's Islamic extremists.

MOROCCO AND EUROPE

Europe considers Morocco a barrier against extremist Islamic groups and an ally among Muslim countries. The European Union has an accord with Morocco to permit the free movement of capital, liberalize trade by establishing an industrial free-trade area, and eventually eliminate customs duties. The accord provides financial aid to Morocco to help with economic, social, and cultural programs. The EU has also promised funds if Morocco attempts to stop

The relationship between Spain and Morocco is tense. In recent years the two countries have disagreed over immigration, the Spanish enclaves in North Africa, oil exploration in disputed waters, and the Western Sahara. In the summer of 2002 a small uninhabited island off the coast of Morocco was the site of another dispute. Ownership of the island (called Perejil by the Spanish and Leila by Moroccans) is disputed. Spain claims it has owned the island since 1668, although there has been no Spanish presence there for the last 40 years; Morocco says it took possession of the island when the Spanish protectorate ended in 1956. On July 10, 2002, Moroccan troops occupied the island, saying they wanted to use it as an outpost to stop smuggling of drugs and illegal immigrants across the Strait of Gibraltar. The Moroccans were soon forced off by Spanish soldiers. This July 17, 2002, photograph shows Moroccans protesting this Spanish action, with the island in the background. With the help of U.S. secretary of state Colin Powell, a diplomatic solution was reached in late July 2002; both countries agreed to leave the tiny island uninhabited.

illegal immigration and the extensive smuggling of consumer items and illegal drugs through the Spanish enclaves to Europe.

Dwindling fish stocks have led Morocco to place occasional bans on European trawlers in its waters. Morocco's relationship with Spain has been strained not only by the fishing dispute but also by territorial and immigration conflicts over the Spanish enclaves of Ceuta and Melilla.

Immigration is perhaps the biggest single issue in Moroccan-EU relations. Europe is only about 8 miles (13 km) away from Morocco. This makes northern Morocco a popular jumping-off point for illegal immigrants to Spain and Europe. In Melilla, police patrol two high metal fences that keep out Moroccans, Algerians, and Africans who want to slip illegally into Europe to find work. Every night men try to climb the barrier to reach Spanish territory, a gateway to the other countries in Europe. Moroccans and others will also travel to Tangier, from which they attempt to cross the Strait of Gibraltar to Spain in small, motorized rafts. Many have died during this dangerous voyage.

In July 2002, tensions flared when Morocco occupied an uninhabited island claimed by Spain. Moroccan officials said they needed the island as a base against illegal immigration.

CHRONOLOGY

ca. 1200 B.C.: Phoenicians arrive on Morocco's northern coast.

500–400 B.C.: Carthaginians arrive in Morocco.

146 B.C.: Romans take Carthage during the Third Punic War.

25 B.C.–A.D. 23: Juba II rules the Kingdom of Mauritania; Berber-Roman civilization begins to flourish in present-day Morocco.

633: A year after the death of Muhammad, Islamic armies emerge from the Arabian Peninsula and begin conquering and converting surrounding lands.

703: Moussa ibn Noceir claims all of Morocco; Islam begins to spread slowly through Morocco.

788: The Idrissid dynasty, Morocco's first Islamic dynasty, begins with reign of Sultan Idriss ben Abdallah.

789: Fez, which becomes the capital of the Idrissid dynasty, is founded.

1055: The Almoravid dynasty begins after the collapse of the Idrissid dynasty.

1062: Marrakech, the Almoravid capital, is founded.

1130–1269: Almohad dynasty.

1269–1465: Marinid dynasty.

1465–1549: Wattasid dynasty.

1525–1659: Sa'adian dynasty.

1644: Moulay Rachid becomes the first Alawite sultan; the Alawite dynasty continues to rule Morocco today.

1672–1727: reign of Sultan Moulay Ismail, who establishes capital in Meknès.

1769: Sultan Sidi ben Abdallah develops port city of Essaouira.

1777: Sidi ben Abdallah becomes one of the first heads of state to recognize American independence.

1786: United States and Morocco sign the Treaty of Marrakech.

1830: Algeria becomes a French colony.

1912: Fez Convention establishes Morocco as a French protectorate; also establishes French, Spanish, and international zones; French resident general Lyautey begins 13-year administration, with Moulay Youssef as sultan.

1919: Abd al-Karim begins rebellion in the Spanish-held Rif.

CHRONOLOGY

1927: Mohammed V begins reign, which will last until 1961 (with a two-year exile between 1953 and 1955).

1956: Morocco achieves its independence on March 2.

1960: An earthquake on February 29 severely damages Agadir and kills about 12,000 people.

1961: King Hassan II begins his reign.

1975: During the Green March, 350,000 Moroccans cross into disputed Spanish (Western) Sahara.

1999: King Hassan II dies on July 23, is succeeded by Mohammed VI.

2000: Morocco's Association Agreement with the European Union begins; King Mohammed VI makes state visit to the United States.

2002: UN-sponsored referendum in Western Sahara is again postponed, indefinitely.

2003: The Arab League meets in Bahrain.

abdicate—to give up or renounce a throne.

Berber—a member of any of various peoples that have long inhabited North Africa in the area west of Tripoli, Libya; also the language of these peoples.

bidonville—a shantytown or slum on the outskirts of a city in North Africa.

corsairs—pirates, especially those operating armed private ships licensed by a government to attack foreign shipping.

couscous—the national dish of Morocco, consisting of small grains of steamed semolina served with a stew; also the semolina grain that is used in the stew.

enclave—a distinct territorial, cultural, or social unit enclosed within a foreign country.

fantasias—in Morocco, mock military exercises conducted on horseback and performed during celebrations or for tourists.

gross domestic product (GDP)—the total value of goods and services produced in a country in a one-year period.

henna—a plant from which is made a red-orange dye used to decorate the hands and feet and color the hair.

indigenous—native or original to a particular area.

Islamist—a Muslim who advocates creation of a society and government that conforms to extremely conservative Islamic doctrine.

jihad—in Islam, a holy war—that is, one undertaken to defend the Muslim religion.

madrassa—a school or college for Islamic studies.

Maghreb—the area that includes the North African countries of Morocco, Algeria, and Tunisia and is often said to include northwest Libya.

manifesto—a written statement declaring publicly the views or intentions of the person or group that issues it.

marabout—a Muslim holy man or saint in Africa.

medina—the original, oldest, or non-European part of a North African city.

Moulay—the title given to an Arab ruler who is a descendant of the prophet Muhammad or a saint; if his name is Mohammed, the title Sidi is used.

moussem—a festival held to honor a marabout, or holy man.

GLOSSARY

oases—isolated fertile areas in a desert that are made possible by a reliable source of water.

plateau—a flat expanse of land at elevation.

qadi—a judge who administers Islamic law.

Qur'an—Islam's holiest book, which the faithful believe consists of God's revelations to the prophet Muhammad; also spelled "Koran."

referendum—a popular vote for the purpose of deciding a public issue rather than electing political representatives.

sharif—a descendant of Muhammad through the Prophet's daughter Fatima; the plural is "shurafa."

Sidi—a title given to a ruler who claims descent from a Muslim saint or from Islam's founder and whose name is also Muhammad or Mohammed.

sirocco—a strong, dry, dusty desert wind.

souk—a marketplace in North Africa or the Middle East.

sultan—in earlier times, the ruler of an Islamic state.

FURTHER READING

Cross, Mary. *Morocco: Sahara to the Sea*. New York: Abbeville Press Publishers, 1995.

Dennis, Lisl, and Dennis Landt. *Living in Morocco*. Great Britain: Clarkson N. Potter, 1992.

Fernea, Elizabeth Warnock. *A Street in Marrakech*. New York: Anchor Press/Doubleday, 1976.

Jereb, James. *Arts and Crafts of Morocco*. San Francisco: Chronicle Books, 1996.

Mann, Vivian B., ed. *Morocco: Jews and Art in a Muslim Land*. London: Merrell Publishers Ltd., in association with the Jewish Museum of New York, 2000.

Mernissi, Fatima. *Dreams of Trespass: Tales of a Harem Girlhood*. New York: Addison-Wesley Publishing Co., 1994.

Oufkir, Malika, and Michele Fitoussi. *Stolen Lives: Twenty Years in a Desert Jail*. New York: Hyperion/Talk Miramax Books, 2000.

Wharton, Edith. *In Morocco*. New Jersey: Ecco Books, 1996 (first published 1919, Charles Scribner's Sons).

Wolfert, Paula. *Couscous and Other Good Foods from Morocco*. New York: Harper & Row, 1973.

INTERNET RESOURCES

http://www.mincom.gov.ma/

Website of the Moroccan Ministry of Culture and Communications. This is a good site for general information about all aspects of the country.

http://www.morocco.com/

Good source of links to Moroccan news and culture; includes photo gallery of Morocco.

http://www.maroc.net/

Links to Radio Casablanca, sports information, popular culture. In English and French.

http://www.arab.net/

Website with links to news articles about current events in the Arab world.

http://www.onlymorocco.com/

A travel website with interesting cultural links.

http://www.i-cias.com/morocco

Titled "Adventures in Morocco," a travel site with good photos and information about Moroccan cities.

http://www.moroccoweb.com/

Informative Moroccan site, especially for history, politics, and business.

Numbers in **bold italic** refer to captions.

INDEX

INDEX

PICTURE CREDITS

The FOREIGN POLICY RESEARCH INSTITUTE (FPRI) served as editorial consultants for the MODERN MIDDLE EAST NATIONS series. FPRI is one of the nation's oldest "think tanks." The Institute's Middle East Program focuses on Gulf security, monitors the Arab-Israeli peace process, and sponsors an annual conference for teachers on the Middle East, plus periodic briefings on key developments in the region.

Among the FPRI's trustees is a former Secretary of State and a former Secretary of the Navy (and among the FPRI's former trustees and interns, two current Undersecretaries of Defense), not to mention two university presidents emeritus, a foundation president, and several active or retired corporate CEOs.

The scholars of FPRI include a former aide to three U.S. Secretaries of State, a Pulitzer Prize–winning historian, a former president of Swarthmore College and a Bancroft Prize–winning historian, and two former staff members of the National Security Council. And the FPRI counts among its extended network of scholars— especially its Inter-University Study Groups—representatives of diverse disciplines, including political science, history, economics, law, management, religion, sociology, and psychology.

DR. HARVEY SICHERMAN is president and director of the Foreign Policy Research Institute in Philadelphia, Pennsylvania. He has extensive experience in writing, research, and analysis of U.S. foreign and national security policy, both in government and out. He served as Special Assistant to Secretary of State Alexander M. Haig Jr. and as a member of the Policy Planning Staff of Secretary of State James A. Baker III. Dr. Sicherman was also a consultant to Secretary of the Navy John F. Lehman Jr. (1982–1987) and Secretary of State George Shultz (1988).

A graduate of the University of Scranton (B.S., History, 1966), Dr. Sicherman earned his Ph.D. at the University of Pennsylvania (Political Science, 1971), where he received a Salvatori Fellowship. He is author or editor of numerous books and articles, including *America the Vulnerable: Our Military Problems and How to Fix Them* (FPRI, 2002) and *Palestinian Autonomy, Self-Government and Peace* (Westview Press, 1993). He edits *Peacefacts*, an FPRI bulletin that monitors the Arab-Israeli peace process.

LYNDA COHEN CASSANOS was born in Baltimore, Maryland, and now lives in New York City with her husband and two children. A children's book editor and freelance writer, she has long been fascinated by Morocco and has visited there several times.